Inspirations for GRAMMAR

Published by Scholastic Ltd,
Villiers House,
Clarendon Avenue,
Leamington Spa,
Warwickshire CV32 5PR

© 1994 Scholastic Ltd
Text © 1994 George Hunt
Revised 1995

Written by George Hunt
Edited by Kate Banham
Designed by Tracey Ramsey
Series designed by Juanita Puddifoot
Illustrated by Linzi Henry
Cover design by Sue Limb
Cover artwork by Ann Johns
Scottish attainment target chart
prepared by Gill Friel

Designed using Aldus Pagemaker
Processed by Pages Bureau,
Leamington Spa
Artwork by Liz Preece,
Castle Graphics, Kenilworth
Printed in Great Britain by
Ebenezer Baylis & Son, Worcester

British Library Cataloguing in Publication Data
A catalogue record for this book is available from the British Library.

ISBN 0-590-53515-3 2nd revised edition
(ISBN 0-590-53138-7 1st edition)

The right of George Hunt to be identified as the Author of this Work has been asserted by him in accordance with the Copyright, Designs and Patent Act 1988.

All rights reserved. This book is sold subject to the condition that it shall not, by way of trade or otherwise, be lent, hired out or otherwise circulated without the publisher's prior consent in any form of binding or cover other than that in which it is published and without a similar condition, including this condition, being imposed upon the subsequent purchaser.

No part of this publication may be reproduced, stored in a retrieval system, or transmitted, in any form or by any means, electronic, mechanical, photocopying, recording or otherwise, without the prior permission of the publisher, except where photocopying for educational purposes within a school or other educational establishment is expressly permitted in the text.

The author would like to thank the children and staff of Brindishe and Annandale Primary Schools in south east London, and of Marigot, Bense and Atkinson schools in Dominica, where many of the ideas presented in this book were tried out.

CONTENTS

Introduction		5
Chapter 1	*Investigating letter strings*	21
Chapter 2	*Words and meanings*	47
Chapter 3	*Investigating phrases and sentences*	77
Chapter 4	*Written texts*	111
Chapter 5	*Oral discourse*	149
Chapter 6	*Language diversity and standard English*	175
Chapter 7	*Assessment and record keeping*	193
Chapter 8	*Bibliography*	199
Scottish attainment target chart		202
Photocopiable pages		203

INTRODUCTION

Grammar

Grammar is one of the most evocative words in the whole of our educational vocabulary. For many teachers the word will arouse memories of a dishwater diet of drills and exercises, the underlining of parts of speech in contrived sentences and the rote learning of a terminology that appeared to have no use beyond the stultifying lessons in which it was taught. To other people, grammar suggests discipline, rigour and correctness; a no-nonsense approach to education, based on teaching children healthy habits of speech, writing, thought and behaviour.

Somewhere between these two positions, there are many teachers who are increasingly curious and uneasy about this term. They are loath to abandon imaginative and purposeful writing activities in favour of arid exercises, yet they worry about the best way of translating into practice the National Curriculum requirement that all children should learn to use standard English. Many of the questions that they ask bear witness to this uncertainty:

- What is the relationship between traditional grammar and the kind of 'language study' demanded by the National Curriculum?
- Can knowledge about language be developed without recourse to workbooks and drills? If it can, what are the alternative resources?
- What is the relationship between speech patterns and writing?
- How should issues of grammatical 'correctness' be dealt with?
- How do we teach children to incorporate standard English into their writing without disparaging their own dialects?
- How much emphasis should be given to linguistic terminology? Is it useful to teach the traditional parts of speech? What about the more recent linguistic terminology that has entered educational discourse via the National Curriculum?
- Traditional grammar takes the sentence as the basic unit of analysis. How do we teach children to build sentences into coherent descriptions, reports, narratives and so on?

This book is not meant to be a course in grammar but a set of ideas for inspiring children with a curiosity about language, while helping teachers to identify their own starting points for investigations into language. The aims of the following chapters and the assumptions about language and learning on which they are based are outlined below.

Aims

- To stimulate curiosity about the forms and functions of spoken and written language.
- To help children become more confident and inventive in their use of language.
- To introduce children to the use of standard English while informing them about the historical roots of this dialect and the attitudes that have grown up around it.
- To enable children to present an informed defence of their own use of language against prejudicial attack.

Assumptions

- Language study should start from what children can do. All speakers of English have a sound *intuitive* grasp of grammar. In enabling children to make this knowledge explicit, we should help them to build on their own language and the language that surrounds them, rather than analysing arbitrary examples.
- From an early age, children are fascinated by language play of all kinds. Teachers will be familiar with the child's natural tendency to play with sounds through rhyme, alliteration and tongue twisters, with spelling patterns through secret codes, with words through puns, riddles, nonsense coinages and jargon, and with longer patterns of language through jokes, storytelling and playground oral rituals. This enjoyment of language games can be built upon in teaching them about grammar and spelling.
- Children learn best when their work is purposeful and when they know that they are working towards goals that satisfy their own needs. Therefore, language study should take place within a context aimed at genuine communicative uses of language rather than decontextualised exercises.

- Language is a social phenomenon that suffuses all aspects of our culture. The media, the languages of street, home and playground are all resources through which children can learn more about how language works.
- Language diversity is both a right and a resource. Children's competence in non-standard dialects and in languages other than English should be respected and used as the basis for developing a critical awareness of language diversity.
- Children learn in what Frank Smith has called 'an environment of demonstrations'. Shared writing and involving children in literature are particularly effective ways of enabling children to extend their own linguistic repertoires.
- Parsing, underlining of parts of speech and decontextualised gap-filling exercises have been discredited. No suggestions for such activities will be made.

A short history of English grammar instruction

In 1762, just over a hundred years before the Forster Education Act of 1870, whose aim was 'to bring elementary education within the reach of every English home, aye, and within reach of those children who have no homes', Bishop Robert Lowth published *A Short Introduction to English Grammar*. This book was to have an enormous effect on the teaching of English throughout the public school system and, after 1870, throughout all other schools as well.

Lowth was alarmed at the fluidity in English spelling, vocabulary and usage which, although always a feature of the language, had begun to accelerate during the Renaissance, due in part to the greater openness of English to the languages of other

Grammar

cultures. (It is this openness which gives much of Shakespeare's language its richness.) The prescription of Lowth and his successors was to lay down rules for 'correct' usage, frequently based on the structures of Latin, which was held to be a language superior to English. It is important to note that Lowth's dictums, for example his formulation of the rule that sentences should not end in prepositions, are based on the contempt of one man for the rhythms of natural speech, rather than on anything intrinsic to the usage itself.

Lowth's legacy of trying to establish 'correct usage' through memorisation of rules, labelling of parts of speech and analysis of sentences remained dominant in schools until the 1950s and 1960s. By then, many teachers regarded these practices as stultifying and counter-productive, and research evidence was beginning to accumulate to support this view. From then on, the teaching of traditional grammar fell out of favour in most primary schools.

However, some educationalists became concerned that children were leaving school without any capacity for analytical reflection on the language surrounding them throughout their lives. Traditionalists yearned for a return to an insistence on correctness. More radical teachers recognised the need for children to become critically aware of the spoken and written texts influencing their lives. In either case, there was a felt need for teachers to start encouraging children to look *at* language rather than just expressing themselves *through* language.

In 1984 HMI published *English 5–16*, which advocated the teaching of knowledge about language, including traditional terminology. Professional responses to this document were largely hostile because of fears that it would lead to a return to the 'grammar grind'. A committee of enquiry, chaired by Professor Kingman, was set up to formulate a 'model' of English which might inform teachers' work in the area of knowledge about language. The committee reported in 1988, advocating that pupils should be taught about language under four broad headings: the forms of the English language, communication and comprehension, language acquisition and development, and historical and geographical variation.

In 1989, building on the work of the Kingman Enquiry, the Cox Report laid the foundations for the English National Curriculum, which came into force in 1990. The statutory orders included knowledge about language in the statements of attainment and programmes of study. While emphasising the need for children to learn to use standard English, they also insisted that they respect their own language and those of others. A return to formal grammar was explicitly ruled out and the teaching of knowledge about language was based on language in use, including playful use.

The revised National Curriculum of 1995, although making more explicit demands for the teaching of standard English, retains the need for language study to be developed in 'an integrated programme of speaking and listening, reading and writing'. It states that 'the richness of dialects and of other languages can make an important contribution to pupils' knowledge and understanding of standard English'.

The scope of grammar

The uneasy curiosity that many teachers feel about grammar may result in part from uncertainties about what the word refers to. Grammar has been defined as a way of taking language apart in order to see how it works, but there are many different ways of doing this. The old-fashioned *prescriptive* grammars of Lowth and his descendants, laying down the law about correct and incorrect usage, have a different function from the sophisticated *descriptive* frameworks of language developed by professional linguists, though there is a confusing overlap in the terminology used. Moreover, these frameworks differ in the way that they divide the language up.

The traditional grammar that many older teachers will remember from their schooldays concerned itself with the relationships between words in sentences (*syntax*). We can, however, look at chunks of language both longer and shorter than a sentence, and take these chunks apart to try to see how they work. For example, words can be analysed into smaller units of meaning such as roots and affixes (*morphology*). Recently, a form of grammar known as *discourse analysis* has attempted to describe the relationships which hold utterances or written sentences together in larger cohesive units. One aspect of this, story grammar, has been used by some teachers to help children to understand the way in which characters, settings and plots combine to form narratives. Another aspect, *conversation analysis*, has been used to show how speakers negotiate meanings and power relations in their spoken interactions. These developments underline the role of meaning in the analysis of language. Traditionally, grammar has confined itself to identifying the rules by which abstract classes of words can be combined into sentences which sound right to native speakers of the language. Descriptive grammars set out in great detail these often very tentative rules, so that linguists can argue about them. Prescriptive grammars have tended to ignore the arguments and the tentativeness, promoting simplified and often arbitrary sets of rules for teachers to drill into children.

Both descriptive and prescriptive grammars have seen language as fixed in time and monolithic in structure. Analysis is confined to the language variety considered to be of high status at the moment, usually in its written form, without any reference to either the reasons why this particular variety has acquired its status, or to the lower-status varieties of language used, most probably, by a much larger number of people.

The activities presented in this book will approach issues of grammatical form through a consideration of the communicative aspects of language. Grammar is presented as the way in which meaning is organised at the level of spelling patterns, words, sentences and more extended chunks of text (paragraphs, poems, stories, descriptions, instructions and so on). In this broad sense, grammar is synonymous with what the National Curriculum refers to as 'language study'. Children will be asked to assess the implications of different word choices and how these choices might vary under the influence of factors such as gender and class. The structure of sentences will be related to what the creator of the sentence is actually trying to do with the form that has been chosen. The origins of some forms of language usage will be investigated and attention focused on the way in which language varies according to who is using it and for what purpose.

Story Grammar

Setting

Characters

Plot

Paradoxically, given that the focus of the book is on the organisation of meaning, many of the activities are based on children's fascination with nonsense and with cryptic distortions of language. This is because our grasp of how to operate the rules for creating language can be sharpened by seeing what happens when we deviate from those rules, much as a cook acquires versatility by departing from the instructions in the recipe and playing about with alternative ingredients.

Linguistic diversity and standard English

A dialect is a social or regional variety of a language which can be identified by distinctive vocabulary or syntactic features. For example, a Lancashire speaker who says, 'Pass cards and I'll show thee how to shuffle' has used distinctive vocabulary (*thee*, which is archaic in standard English, instead of *you*) and a distinctive syntactic form (omission of the definite article *the* before *cards*).

Accent refers only to the way in which words are pronounced and the 'tune' of the sentence. This is theoretically separable from dialect; it would, after all, be possible to say the sentence above in a 'posh' Southern accent. (In discussing the difference between accent and dialect with children, it might be worthwhile asking why such an utterance would sound rather incongruous.)

Standard English started life as a regional dialect of the Midlands. For various historical and political reasons, described in more detail on pages 175–177, it has become the dialect of commerce, government and education. It can be spoken in any accent, though, historically, the one most closely associated with it is Received Pronunciation, often described as *BBC English*. The vast majority of all publications in English are written in this dialect and it has become the world's foremost international language. However, it has been estimated that only ten per cent of the population speak in this dialect at home, and only one per cent do so in Received Pronunciation (Richard Hudson, *Teaching Grammar*, 1992, Blackwell). The fact that most people associate 'correctness' only with this variety of English shows how successfully it has been promoted as the standard against which all other varieties must be judged.

This writer believes that social and regional dialects should be respected and children's achievements in such dialects be used as the foundation for further linguistic development. The very presence of a variety of languages, dialects and accents in a classroom provides a rich source for reflection and research. Our main object is to help children to delight in language and to use it more flexibly. Trying to achieve this by criticising the language of their home or peer group would be like trying to roast a turkey by putting it in the fridge.

As the Kingman Report advises, issues surrounding the use of standard English should be subjected to explicit discussion. Children should be made aware that standard English still retains a powerful gatekeeping function in our society, as well as being an indispensable medium for written and international communication. All children should therefore be given opportunities to learn about standard English and how to use it. In the words of the Cox Report, 'The aim is to add standard English to the repertoire, not to replace other dialects or languages.'

All of the above points concerning the achievements of speakers of non-standard dialects apply equally well to those children who come to school speaking languages other than English. Recent research has shown that bilingual children can develop greater insights into language than monolingual children, since they are able to observe linguistic phenomena from the vantage points of two (or more) languages. If their achievements are respected, the knowledge about language that they can bring into the classroom will be a valuable resource for all learners.

Linguistic terminology

According to the Cox Report, the purpose of teaching children a special vocabulary about language is to 'consolidate what is already known intuitively'. In getting children to reflect on language use, we need a set of terms for important concepts, just as we need them in any other curriculum area. The danger is that once a set of terms has been identified, teachers will attempt to teach them by rote, without any demonstration of their usefulness. It is this threat of a return to drill and parsing that causes many teachers to reel away in horror from any attempt at all to teach children the names of parts of speech, for example.

Reducing grammar to drills in the identification of parts of speech is as impoverishing as reducing cookery instruction to the rote learning of the names of the utensils to be used. Nevertheless, just as we would not want our cookery students to refer to a pressure cooker as one of those big pans you use steam to cook things quickly in, we should spare children the inconvenience of using circumlocutions for those components of language we will want to discuss in some of the following activities. Linguistic terminology should be learned in contexts which require the use of a special vocabulary.

Grammar **13**

It should also be stressed that the appropriate terminology should not be confined to the names of parts of speech. The traditional definitions attached to these terms are problematic, as we shall later see, and they do not get us very far in discussing how language is used in real situations. Opportunities will arise for the use of other terms related to some of these situations: *accent* and *dialect* when discussing language diversity, for example, or *euphemism* and *bias* when discussing persuasive uses of texts.

One circumstance which makes the teacher's job easier is that, in general, children like to collect terminology, and will latch on to a new and rich-sounding word with the same enthusiasm that they would pick up any other kind of interesting object.

Talking and writing

In recent years, speaking has enjoyed something of a renaissance in classrooms. Research studies such as the Bristol Language Development Project have emphasised the role of speaking in establishing educational foundations for children, while the work of the National Oracy Project has demonstrated its crucial role in learning across the curriculum. The inclusion of Speaking and Listening as Attainment Target 1 in the English National Curriculum has also been seen as a sign of the acceptance of classroom talk as indispensable rather than regrettable.

This acceptance is long overdue. It has often been pointed out that while people have been talking to each other for as long as the human race has existed, writing is a relatively recent invention. It is therefore ironic that writing has been regarded by traditional grammarians as a 'purer' mode of language. This is probably because most instances of speech are spontaneous. Conversations are made up between participants as they go along, so speech tends to be full of false starts, overlaps, corrections, hesitations, interruptions, deviations, redundant remarks and 'keep going' utterances such as *you know*, *erm*, *uh-huh*, *I mean*, and so on. In the case of most types of writing, these formative processes have taken place before the reader looks at the text, which gives writing an appearance of far greater tidiness than speech. It would be a mistake to conclude from this that writing is more 'grammatical' than talking, or that we should strive to base speech on the more formal rhythms of written language. Even if this were possible, it could only create the kind of stilted dialogue reminiscent of a badly written soap opera. Speech, including the speech of highly educated speakers of standard English, is *essentially* messy, as an examination of any transcript of recorded spontaneous conversation will show.

The kind of children's talk that accompanies learning activities in the classroom is rarely expressed in polished sentences or in standard English. This is as it should be. 'Talk for learning' is essentially interactive and will inevitably contain all the markers of spontaneity, contest and negotiation mentioned above. Its heterogeneity in terms of accent and dialect reflects the linguistic diversity of our children. Attempting to impose some narrow definition of correctness on this flux is likely to be both futile and suffocating.

For this reason, it is recommended that children should learn about standard English forms through their reading, and through the models of speech surrounding them in the classroom and through the media. They should be given the opportunity to practise such forms in their writing, where they are better able to reflect on language choices, before they are expected to use these forms confidently in speech.

The activities in this book maintain the valuable links between speech and writing. Some of the differences between these two modes are suggested as starting points for classroom research. Much use is made of shared writing, with the teacher acting as a scribe for children composing orally. Though the differences between standard and non-standard forms are explored through both spoken and written texts, it is through writing (and forms of speech that approximate to writing, such as the planned and semi-planned dialogues of drama and role-play) that children are encouraged to incorporate standard forms into their own patterns of language.

Organising the teaching of grammar

There are at least four ways of organising the teaching of grammar in the primary school.

1. *Purely incidentally.* In this case, the teacher introduces the child or class to new concepts as and when opportunities arise. For example, a teacher might talk about the need for more complex (or simpler) sentence structures while discussing a particular piece of work with an individual child or group. She might talk about metaphor after reading a poem or story in which this device plays a part. A misleading or inflammatory headline in a morning paper might provide a topical opportunity to discuss how the shaping of language can be used to disinform.

The advantage of this approach is that it keeps the study of language very close to children's everyday concerns. Through reading and writing conferences, and in the intimacy of the class story or sharing time, concepts can be introduced and related to current experience very directly. However, if this approach is used exclusively, it becomes difficult to ensure that children experience a sufficiently broad spectrum of issues and activities. It would probably be more effective for the teacher to maintain this approach alongside a more structured programme of investigations.

2. *As an explicit strand within a topic.* This can be a good way of ensuring that a range of appropriate issues are dealt with from week to week, while using the involvement of the children in a cross-curricular topic to maintain relevance and interest. Topics centred on historical or geographical subjects provide an excellent background for the discussion

of language change and diversity. Topics based on themes from mathematics, science or technology yield opportunities for research into specialised vocabulary and subject-specific genres.

3. *As an explicit strand not related to other topics.* This is probably the most straightforward way of ensuring that an inventory of grammar topics is given regular attention, but it is also most likely to produce decontextualised exercises, particularly if teachers become reliant on structured schemes or workbooks which do not relate the tasks to the children's current concerns. The work done in such sessions could therefore prove to be a waste of time, involving children in isolated exercises when they could be using their energies to do something more creative.

However, there is a case for giving children short, daily activities in which they are persuaded to reflect on the anatomy of language, without necessarily relating these activities to ongoing work. This can be done through language games which might, for example, be played when the children first come into class, or during a designated time between longer sessions, or they might form a resource that children turn to when they have finished other work. You will be aware that only a fine line distinguishes a language game from a language exercise, and much

will depend on the atmosphere that the teacher creates when introducing these activities. The teacher must also balance the need for such games to be kept reasonably brisk, against the need to allow time for reflection on what has been learned.

4. *As the focus of a topic.* Devoting an entire term or half a term to projects such as 'Languages in our school', 'Word games', 'Playground rhymes and songs', or 'Communication' is an excellent way of generating

Grammar 17

curiosity about language, pulling in contributions from families and the community at large and involving children in some extended research. The only drawback to this approach lies in the possibility that it might lead to a tokenistic attitude. If children have covered some aspect of knowledge about language in depth at one point in their school careers, some teachers might neglect other aspects when struggling to plan the 'delivery' of an overloaded curriculum. Issues need to be revisited. 'They did language diversity in year four' is no reason not to 'do' it in as many ways as possible throughout the rest of the children's education.

Perhaps the best way of organising language study is to teach it as an explicit strand within all cross curricular topics, supplementing this with short, regular bouts of 'linguistic gymnastics' (games and other short activities based on current concerns) and less frequent but more in-depth investigations of particular issues in language. Incidental talk about such issues, in the context of the children's own work and observations, is also very important.

How to use this book

Each chapter in the book provides background information for the teacher, followed by practical activities arranged in order of difficulty. The chapters themselves are *not* arranged in order of difficulty. The first four proceed from a discussion of letter strings and morphology, through material on words and sentences, to an examination of more extended chunks of spoken and written text. The later chapters deal with issues related to whole texts. This is an organising device for sequencing the teacher information sections, and should not be seen to imply a developmental sequence or instructional plan. From their earliest attempts at both speech and writing, children appear to operate from all levels of the scale at once, enjoying the cadences of story and conversation while striving to find stable forms for the smallest units of such texts. When these children have become highly skilled language users, they may still find it interesting and instructive to investigate the patterning of these small units, as well as the overall structure of the texts that they occur in.

So, within the first chapter on letter strings there are activities appropriate for both emergent and fluent readers and writers. Similarly, the fact that the chapter on language diversity comes later in the book does not imply that this type of language investigation is suitable only for more skilled readers and writers. From the earliest stages of education we can encourage children to reflect on who creates the messages in our environment, and why they take the form that they do. I have tried to highlight ways such awareness might be fostered throughout the book.

Because of the fuzziness of categories like word and sentence, and the essentially recursive nature of language learning, there is an inevitable amount of permeability between chapters, and a lot of referencing backwards and forwards. I see this as a strength, reinforcing the idea that children use all levels of language simultaneously, and that linguistic skills and concepts need to be revisited and refined.

There are two main ways in which teachers might use the activities:
• as a source for compiling the type of language games described in later chapters;
• as a guide for integrating language activities into ongoing work.

The first approach is a straightforward matter of browsing, deciding on what seems interesting and useful, then adapting the activity to the age range in question. I have added a 'curriculum context' note to each activity, to emphasise the need to set it within the ongoing work of the class. This is implicit in the second approach, for which I recommend the following procedure:
1. Look at your scheme of work for the time span you are contemplating and make a list of the types of written and spoken interaction implied by what you have planned.
2. In relation to each item on the list, ask yourself what opportunities exist for developing the following:
• *critical* language awareness (for instance, making children more aware of the social context in which particular texts are created);

Grammar 19

- more extensive knowledge of word structure and vocabulary;
- greater versatility in the construction of spoken and written sentences;
- the ability to read and write texts in a variety of genres;
- awareness of language diversity (including the use of standard English where appropriate).

3. Consult the appropriate section of the book *after* the previous steps, and modify the suggested activities in accordance with the needs and interests of the children and the content of the topic.

Particular attention needs to be paid to the time factor. Some game-type activities which might be enjoyable and instructive if indulged in for ten to fifteen minutes could prove to be crushingly drudgerous if dragged out to the length of a lesson.

Conversely, there are other activities requiring lengthy research, discussion and revisiting. Suggested time allocations are given within the 'Curriculum context' note.

Shared writing

Several of the activities suggest a shared writing approach. This entails the teacher acting as scribe while the children orally compose various types of text. When a first draft has been created, usually on a large format, highly visible surface, the teacher can help the children redraft and edit. Shared writing is a valuable technique for the type of work offered here, since it enables the teacher to focus the children's attention on specific aspects of language while retaining the children's own compositions as the basis from which to work. For example, children who have dictated a story for a class anthology can be encouraged to choose ways of trimming, expanding, recombining or resequencing its sentences, with the teacher providing suggestions.

The 'shared writing materials' refers to felt-tipped pens, flipcharts, board, chalk, A1 paper, OHP transparencies and whatever else is appropriate for your classroom and the size of group you are working with. The important thing is that each member of the group should have a clear view of what you write.

CHAPTER 1

Investigating letter patterns

English spelling is complicated, even though it is based on a seemingly simple principle. This is the alphabetical principle: for each sound (or phoneme) in a spoken word, there is one printed symbol (or grapheme) that represents it in writing. A grapheme may consist of one or more letters. The fact that English adheres only loosely to this principle makes learning how to spell fairly difficult but also provides a wealth of information about the development and workings of the language.

Several factors have contributed to the complexity of the relationships between sound and spelling in English, perhaps the most fundamental one being the mismatch between the number of phonemes in the spoken language and the number of graphemes available for writing. English contains about 44 separate speech sounds. The inventory differs according to dialect; there are sounds in Liverpudlian English, for example, which do not occur in Received Pronunciation, and vice versa. Written English attempts to represent these sounds using just 26 letters. Consequently, many sounds have to be represented by a combination of letters.

Various historical influences have caused further complications. After the Norman conquest, French became the language of the upper classes in England, and French scribes assumed positions of power in the Church and in education. Their influence led to radical changes in conventions for spelling English words. For example, *z*, *g* and *q* were introduced, and *o* replaced *u* in many words because of the confusion caused by continental style handwriting. Thus, Old English *cween* became *queen*, and *sunu*, *cuman* and *lufu* evolved into *son, come* and *love*.

The introduction of printing in 1476 prompted the process of standardising spelling, though it also added further complications. As many of the early printers were not native speakers of English (many of them were Dutch), they used their own spelling conventions to represent English sounds.

The development of printing began during the early stages of 'The Great Vowel Shift', a dramatic change in the way that English was pronounced. In Chaucer's time, the word *moon*, for example, would have been pronounced with a long *o* sound, similar to the way in which moan is pronounced today in Northern English dialects. The double *o* in this word reflects its earlier pronunciation. This evolution towards modern pronunciation was not reflected in printing conventions, so many of the spellings that we have today represent the way the language was spoken during its late middle period, rather than the way it is spoken today. Many silent letters, such as the *k* at the beginning of *knee*, the *t* in *castle* and the *w* in *wrong*, are vestiges of the earlier pronunciation of these words.

Other silent letters are due to the meddling of lexicographers. In the 16th century, scholars tried to amend the spelling of many words in order to make their supposed Latin or Greek roots visible. Thus, *receit* acquired a *p* to reflect the Latin *recipere*, and *sutil* a *b* to reflect *subtilis*, resulting eventually in the modern forms *receipt* and *subtle*.

Added to this are the complexities caused by a steady influx of words from other cultures and from the ever expanding terminologies of science and other areas of learning.

The result of all this is a spelling system in which one sound can be represented by several different letters and letter combinations, and in which a letter or letter combination can stand for a variety of different sounds, as demonstrated in Figure 1.

This is a system in which many words *are* spelled according to fairly simple phonic rules, but many others, including those most frequent in everyday speech and writing, are not.

We also have to bear in mind that English spelling reflects grammatical and meaning relationships as well as just the sound of words. For example, the most common way of showing plurality in English is to add *-s* to the noun. In speech, this gives us three separate pronunciation possibilities (see Figure 2).

Similarly, the *-ed* used at the end of a verb to signify the past tense can also be pronounced in at least three different ways (see Figure 3).

The way in which meaning frequently overrules sound in determining how words are spelled can be seen in Figure 4. Here we see how visual patterns shared by meaning-related words differ in their pronunciation.

Because spelling encodes word history and meaning relations, as well as sound, phonological knowledge, though necessary for learning how to spell, is not in itself sufficient. What is needed in addition is knowledge of the *visual* regularities of spelling.

Possible pronunciations of printed letter 'o'	Possible ways of spelling sound 'o' (as in *old*)	
gold	chauffeur	brooch
women	chateau	soul
once	Yeoville	though
do	sew	apropos
fog	gold	depot
correct	oats	shadow
London	hoe	
won	note	

Figure 1

Singular	Plural	Pronunciation
cat	cats	cat[s]
dog	dogs	dog[z]
horse	horses	horse[iz]

Figure 2

Present	Past	Pronunciation
roll	rolled	roll[d]
walk	walked	walk[t]
depend	depended	depend[id]

Figure 3

Variation in pronunciation	Examples
Variation in the sound of a consonant	medicine medical
	criticise critical
Variation in the sound of a vowel	divide division
	phone phonic
Silent/sounded variation	muscle muscular
	sign signal
	soften soft

Figure 4

Spelling development

In *SPEL is a four letter word* (1987, Scholastic), Richard Gentry identifies five overlapping stages that most children go through in learning how to spell.

1. Pre-communicative: random letters and other signs are used in attempts to express meaning.

2. Semi-phonetic: the child is acquiring the concept that letters stand for sounds. Abbreviated forms occur (*skl* for *school*) and initial letters are sometimes used to represent whole words.

3. Phonetic: the child is now operating on a firm sound-symbol basis, reflecting a consistent but simplistic view of how spelling works. Many words will be misspelled as a result (*ate* for *eighty*, *nabuz* for *neighbours*).

4. Transitional: there is a developing realisation that spelling involves more than sound-symbol relationships. Spellings begin to reflect the accepted letter strings of English, but with incomplete mastery of these conventions (*nihte* for *night*, *beutifull* for *beautiful*).

5. Correct: the writer now has firm control over the different factors involved in spelling and is sufficiently familiar with visual letter strings to know when a word doesn't 'look right'.

Phonological knowledge can only take a child to the third stage of this development, equivalent to Level 2 of the National Curriculum. In order to progress beyond this, children need to become aware of the other factors underlying spelling. These factors have been described as '...a kind of grammar for letter sequences that generate permissible combinations without regard to sound'. (Gibson and Levin, 1975, in Peters, 1985). In other words, the writer has to develop a feel for the *serial probability* of letter combinations. The fact that some combinations are common in English (*-str-*, *-ion-*, *-sure-*, *-oo-*, *-ach-*) while others are uncommon (*-lmn-*, *-mpt-*, *-bd-*) and some never occur at all (*-bpc-*, *-xgh-*, *-oiuae-*, *-jq-*) enables the experienced writer to judge whether or not an uncertain word looks right.

Peters and Smith (1993) argue that children should develop an awareness of serial probability in the course of purposeful writing activities, practising patterns based on words that occur in their own compositions. The basic principles that they advocate are as follows:

1. Spelling requires a two-pronged approach. Children writing first drafts should not be overly concerned with spelling accuracy, but they should receive, in parallel, instruction in strategies for memorising letter strings. This instruction should take place separately from their writing sessions but should be based on words that the children have attempted to spell in these sessions.

2. Letter strings are visual, not phonic. The string *ove*, for example, occurs with different sound values in words such as *love, stove, remover, hovel* and *Hoover*. Therefore, such patterns need to be practised through a look/cover/write/check technique.

3. Spelling ability is closely linked to fluent handwriting. Children need to be taught a clear, joined-up hand as soon as possible, in order to practise the writing of common letter strings and words containing these strings.

4. Spelling activities should encourage children to pay attention to the internal structure of words, looking at them with a determination to write them correctly.

5. The child's image of himself or herself as a writer is crucial. Activities which inspire curiosity about words and confidence in the ability to master their patterns are essential.

Morpheme patterns

As we saw with the example of the *ove* pattern, letter strings are essentially visual features of words and have no necessary connection with either the sound or the meaning of the words in which they occur. However, there are certain regular letter sequences in written language which do connect with the way in which spellings represent meanings. Knowledge of these regularities might help a learner grasp spelling conventions, as well as contribute to a general familiarity with and curiosity about word structures.

A morpheme is the smallest unit of meaning in language, and may be smaller than a word. For example, in the previous sentence, the word *smallest* consists of two morphemes – the root word

Investigating letter patterns

small and the suffix *-est*. Many words contain only one morpheme; for example, *a*, *word*, *boomerang*. Others contain several; for example, *uncontrollable*, *institutionalise*. Morphemes can be either free or bound. Free morphemes are capable of functioning independently as words; for example, *blacksmith* consists of the two free morphemes, *black* and *smith*. Bound morphemes can only occur embedded in other words; for example, the prefix *un-* in *unhappy* and the suffix *-ly* in *miserably* do not occur in English as independent words.

It is important to note that morphemes are not the same as syllables. For one thing, morphemes can contain any number of syllables. For another, the way in which we divide a word into syllables might not correspond with the way in which it can be divided into morphemes. The word *yellowish*, for example, has three syllables (*yell-/-ow-/-ish*) but only two morphemes (*yellow* and *-ish*). This distinction is important because some authorities on spelling suggest that teachers should encourage children to sound words out into syllables in order to spell them. Although the ability to recognise the syllabic structure of *printed* words has been shown to be an important aspect of fluent reading (Jager Adams, 1990), the division of *spoken* words into syllables as a prelude to attempting to spell them is problematic. If we divide the word *immediately* into spoken syllables, we get something like *im-ee-jut-ly*, which is not a reliable guide to its spelling. However, if we devise activities that draw the children's attention to the root *media* in the written word, relating it to words like *mediate* and *medium*, and showing how the affixes *im-* and *-ly* work, we might be on firmer ground. Similarly, children who spell *really* as *reely* might be helped by being made aware of the root form *real* and related forms like *reality*, *unreal*, *surreal* and so on. In each case, we are encouraging children to look at letter strings which convey predictable meanings (the root words) or which do regular jobs in modifying the meanings of these root words (prefixes and suffixes).

This sort of instruction should be put in its proper context. The rote learning of morphological features is unlikely to do anything but bore the children. If, however, such teaching is initially inspired by the words that children have actually tried to use in their writing and then extended via word games to related patterns in other words, then we have a purposeful context for dealing with immediate needs and for developing longer-term, more general curiosity about words.

We also need to be clear about the relationships between the parallel factors underlying spelling patterns and what these imply for instruction. To summarise:

• *The alphabetic factor.* Children need to be aware that spoken words can be analysed into phonemes and that these phonemes can be represented by written symbols. This is the fundamental principle underlying writing in English and it should be stressed in early literacy activities. However, children also need to learn that although there are reliable sound-symbol relationships in English, it is also the case that a particular sound can be represented in a variety of ways, and a particular letter or group of letters can stand for a variety of sounds, or for no sound at all. The compilation of thematic and personal ABCs is an excellent way of demonstrating this to children.

• *The visual factor.* There are useful regularities in spelling which have nothing to do with either the sound or the meaning of the words in which they occur. Because of the complexity of letter-sound relationships, it is essential that children develop the capacity to memorise and produce common letter strings without recourse to unreliable sounding-out strategies. This should be done through activities which encourage children to look for visual regularities within words, through handwriting practice based on these regularities, and through the use of the look/cover/write/check technique whenever they are writing unfamiliar words. The most crucial time for this type of instruction is when children's phonological knowledge is secure and they are ready to progress beyond the phonetic stage of spelling development. However, this does not mean that such activities should be postponed until this stage. Knowledge of letter strings should develop in parallel with children's phonological knowledge.

• *The morphemic factor.* Some letter strings have a direct link with the meanings of the words in which they occur. Knowledge of such strings is a useful additional aspect of visual awareness, and may lead to enhanced competence in the writing and recognition of words and in the development of poetic language through the creation of new words. Again, activities to develop this awareness need not wait until phonological knowledge is secure. Particularly useful starting points for investigating morphemes are provided by those word families in which morphemes *do* coincide neatly with syllabic structure. Common examples are the *-day* pattern at the end of the names of the days of the week, *-ing* endings on such words as *working* and *walking* and the *-y* suffix at the end of adjectives such as *funny* and *happy*.

Finally, we should also bear in mind that environmental print surrounds children with examples of letters and letter strings which have only indirect or vestigial links to sound and meaning. Examples of this are abbreviations, acronyms, initial letters, registration codes and idiomatic uses like *X-ray*, *B team*, *A to Z* and *Bar-B-Q*.

The activities which follow focus on these areas, while encouraging a general curiosity about word structure.

ACTIVITIES

1. Name spellings

Age range
Five to seven.

Group size
A small or a large group.

What you need
Shared writing materials, Blu-Tack.

Curriculum context
A short talking and writing activity that could be done in the reception class at the beginning of term when the children are getting to know each other.

What to do
Ask each member of the group to write his or her name on a piece of card that can then be stuck on to the easel paper or flip chart. You may need to do the writing for the children. When this has been done, encourage the children to select their own criteria for sorting and re-sorting the names. Obvious categories that might arise are girls' names and boys' names, short names and long names, common names and unusual names.

When the children are accustomed to this, introduce your own criteria for sorting the names and see if the children can identify what they are. Some possibilities are:
• alphabetical ordering;
• arranging names with shared letter strings into columns (see illustration);
• arranging together names that have recognisable smaller words embedded in them (for example, Catherine, Alice, Parminder);
• grouping together names with the same initial letter;
• grouping together names that share the same ending;
• separating monosyllabic and polysyllabic names (children can try counting out the 'beats' within each name).

Further activity
This activity also provides an opportunity for introducing the distinction between upper- and lower-case letters. Names in which the same letter occurs both at the beginning and later on (for example, Robert, Adrian, Leila) may provide a starting point for discussing shape differences between upper- and lower-case letters.

2. Letter strings from names

Age range
Five to seven.

Group size
Small groups, then individuals.

What you need
Cards with the names of the children in the group, individual word lists based on the letter patterns in each name, writing materials.

Curriculum context
Handwriting practice.

What to do
Make illustrated word lists based on letter patterns in the names of the children in the group, as in this example:

Name: Gr<u>ant</u>
Word list: <u>ant</u>, <u>ant</u>elope, gi<u>ant</u>, pl<u>ant</u>, eleph<u>ant</u>, praying m<u>ant</u>is.

(It is best to select words with vivid visual connotations.)

Choose one name card and word list and ask the children to identify the relationship between the name and the words. Help the children to read the words in their own lists, using the picture clues. Demonstrate how the letter string should be written. When this has been done, the children can try to make up sentences orally, combining as many of the words as possible, for example, '*Grant's giant praying mantis ate the antelope and elephant, then a giant ant ate her.*'

You might then like to write these sentences out for the children to illustrate and copy, to provide a personalised context for the practice of particular letter strings, and an introduction to the regularities of spelling.

3. Memorable sentences for letter strings

Age range
Five to eleven.

Group size
Individuals or a small group.

What you need
Writing materials.

Curriculum context
A spelling and handwriting activity which is closely focused on specific individual needs.

What to do
Using the children's previous writing, identify a particular letter string that needs to be practised. Help the child or group to make a list of words which contain the target letter string. Remember that it is not essential that there should be any phonic resemblance between the words, since the objective is to memorise a *visual* pattern. The children, working together or as individuals, should then compose short meaningful sentences using as many of the words as possible, as in this example for the *-ear-* letter string: *'If I hear you swear, it's a thick ear and early to bed, tears or no tears.'*

These sentences can be illustrated and written out by the children, perhaps using large posters. They can then be used as an aid to memorise the spelling patterns with which other children may have had difficulty.

4. Card games with letter strings

Age range
Five to seven.

Group size
A small group, then pairs.

What you need
Blank playing cards, a photocopy of an array of words and words within words for each child.

Curriculum context
A spelling and handwriting activity that can be part of a topic on word games. Older children who need practice in attending to letter strings can prepare the card games for younger children.

What to do
Show the children the array of words and help them to read them. Ask the children to look for visual similarities between the words and to link those that belong together. When this has been done, give the children the blank playing cards so that the words can be neatly copied on to them. The children can then play conventional games with the cards (snap, Pelmanism) or devise new games.

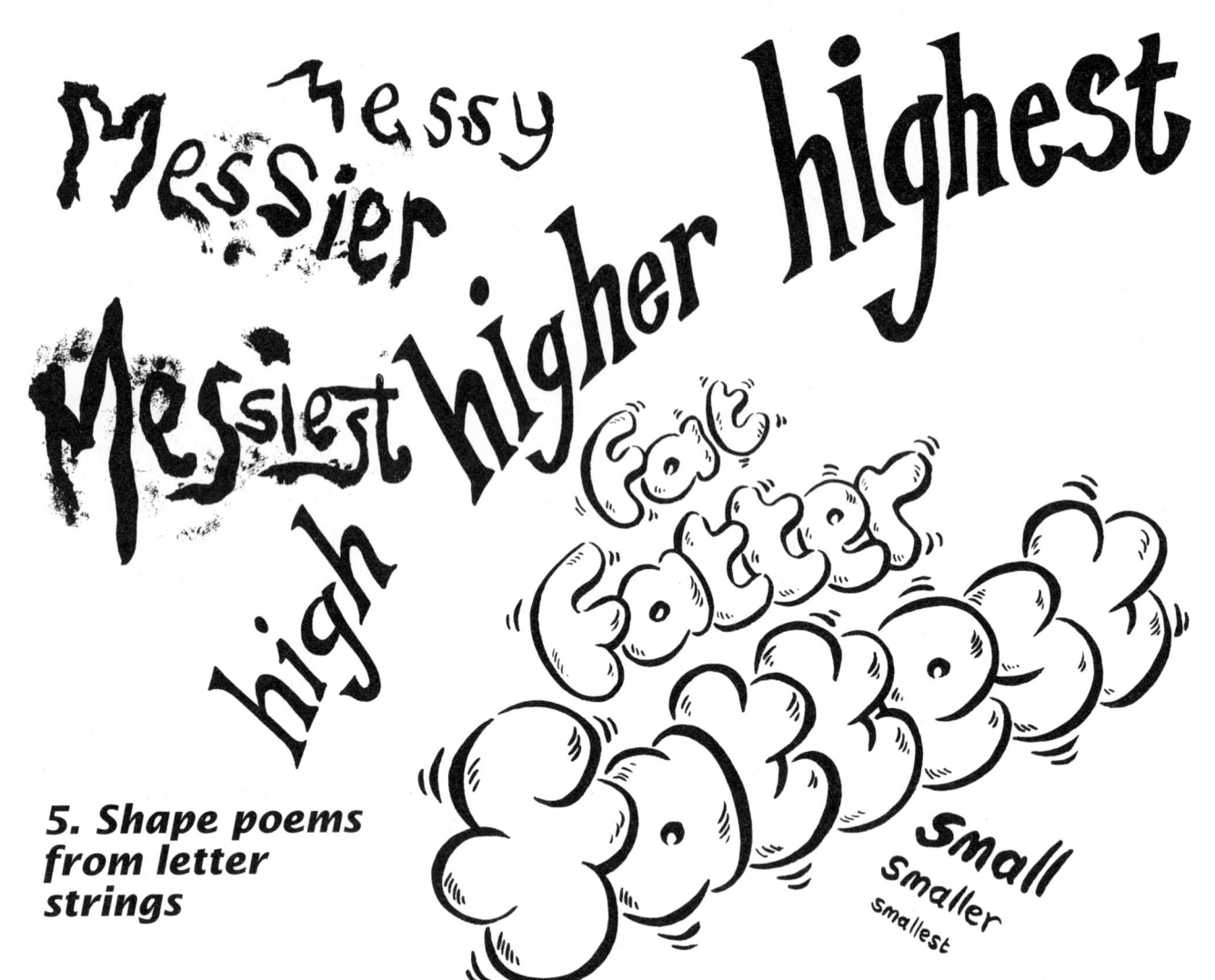

messy
Messier
Messiest
higher
highest
high
fat
fatter
fattest
small
smaller
smallest

5. Shape poems from letter strings

Age range
Five to eleven.

Group size
A small group or the whole class.

What you need
Drawing materials, examples of published shape poems.

Curriculum context
A spelling and handwriting practice activity that can be integrated into art work and creative writing.

What to do
Show the children examples of shape poems. (*Madtail, Miniwhale and Other Shape Poems* edited by Wes Magee, 1991, Penguin, is a good resource for this.) Allow the children plenty of opportunities to compose their own shape poems on self-selected subjects.

Demonstrate how the idea of a shape poem can be used as a way of practising letter strings by visualising the meaning of the words in which they occur. The comparative and superlative forms of adjectives provide a very accessible way of doing this (see illustration).

Allow the children to create their own graphics based on letter patterns.

6. Word webs (1)

Age range
Five to eleven.

Group size
A small group or the whole class.

What you need
Writing materials.

Curriculum context
A quick writing game that could be played at the beginning of the school day or between lessons.

What to do
Write a common letter string on the board. Which one you choose will be determined by the needs of the group. Ask each child to copy the letter string and then to write down as many words as they can think of containing that string. Each child should do his or her own writing, though the group should be encouraged to share ideas and to discuss whether or not particular words fit the pattern. After a given time, you can write the children's words on the board or on an overhead projector as they read them out.

This activity can be developed by giving the group a text such as a newspaper or a story and asking them to scan it for words containing the string. This can be very useful, but it is particularly important that the activity is kept reasonably rapid. You should ensure that the text to be scanned does indeed contain several obvious instances of the letter string. It is also important to ensure that the size of print is appropriate for the children's reading ability.

Further activity
The investigation of letter strings which occur at the beginnings of words will generate a collection of alliterative words (words beginning with the same sound) which can then be used to compose alliterative sentences or tongue twisters (see Activity 8).

7. Thematic ABCs

Age range
Five to eleven.

Group size
A small group or the whole class.

What you need
Writing and book-making materials.

Curriculum context
An open-ended activity to introduce a new topic and to develop dictionary skills and knowledge of vocabulary related to any area.

What to do
At the launch of any new topic with the class, ask the children to brainstorm all the words they know related to that topic. Depending on age and ability, the children can write these words themselves or they can be written by the teacher as part of a shared writing session. You can then help the children to order the words alphabetically and to publish them as illustrated ABCs. As the topic develops, new words can be added. A display of these books next to such conventionally published ABCs as *The Calypso Alphabet* by John Agard, (1989, HarperCollins) would make an attractive classroom resource.

8. Alliterative ABCs

Age range
Five to eleven.

Group size
A small group or the whole class.

What you need
Writing and book-making materials.

Curriculum context
An open-ended activity that can be integrated into topic work or poetry writing.

What to do
Ask the children to brainstorm all the words they know, beginning with a particular letter. This can be done as an individual writing activity or as shared writing. Different groups can be given different letters to work with, or the whole class can be given different letters on different days, and the results compared later. The children should then work together at creating as short a coherent sentence as possible, using as many of the words as they can. (The shorter the sentence, the more concentrated the alliterative effect.)

Encourage the children to look at the sentences and investigate, for each letter, how many of the words have a similar initial *sound*, as well as having the same initial *letter*, and how many have different initial sounds. It will be found that words beginning with consonants are highly alliterative, while words beginning with vowels are much less so.

This activity provides a useful context for a discussion of the vowel/consonant distinction, and offers the children vivid demonstrations of both the simple and the more complicated relationships between letters and sounds.

9. 'Have-a-go' books for spelling patterns

Age range
Five to eleven.

Group size
Individuals.

What you need
Exercise books, pens.

Curriculum context
A routine, self-help strategy for dealing with spelling difficulties while children are editing their work. It can also be used to encourage anxious spellers to 'have a go' at words in writing their first drafts.

What to do
This activity requires the children to understand that the teacher is the final source of help in spelling, rather than the first, and that they should develop routines for helping themselves to spell.

The children should be given exercise books where they try out spellings of which they are unsure. They should then find the correct spellings in a dictionary or by asking a writing partner, teacher or other helper. A suggested format for each page is shown in the illustration.

The correct spelling column should be covered with a card while the child is using the practise column.

Animal sounds	Quiet sounds	Watery sounds
hiss	whisper	splash
caterwaul	sigh	gush
bleat	murmur	gurgle
peewit	tinkle	trickle
bark	rustle	drip

10. Investigating onomatopoeia

Age range
Five to eleven.

Group size
A small group or the whole class.

What you need
Writing materials and texts such as comics, jingles, nursery rhymes, readers from early levels of reading schemes, 'noisy poems', and so on.

Curriculum context
An open-ended investigation, aimed at familiarising children with relationships between spelling, sound and meaning, which can be used in poetry writing.

What to do
Introduce the children to the concept of onomatopoeia through such familiar examples as animal noises (*moo*, *bleat*, *neigh*) or words for loud sounds (*crash*, *boom*, *roar*). After the children have identified the relationship between such words and what they refer to, they will have many examples to contribute themselves. They can then browse through the texts that the teacher has selected, collecting examples of onomatopoeic words and listing them. They may well find interesting examples of words that may or may not be onomatopoeic (see Activity 11). The words can be categorised according to various criteria, as shown above.

The word lists thus created can be used for various extension activities.
- the words can be regrouped across categories according to patterns of alliteration and rhyme;
- Venn diagrams can be created to show the overlap between the listed categories;
- the lists can be used to make onomatopoeic poems – *A Book of Noisy Poems* edited by Jill Bennett (1987, OUP) should provide some inspiration;
- children can extend the lists by making up their own words in different categories.

11. Onomatopoeia?

Age range
Nine to eleven.

Group size
A small group working in pairs.

What you need
Dictionaries, writing materials.

Curriculum context
A short investigation of a less straightforward aspect of sound-spelling-meaning relationships, to interest children who are developing independence in spelling.

What to do
Ask the children to choose a number of familiar words from the *sl-* section of the dictionary and to discuss their definitions. Ask them if any of these words appear to have anything in common. The children will probably spot that words like *slug*, *slither*, *slime*, *slop* and *sly* tend to have rather negative connotations for most people. They could then discuss whether this has anything to do with the sound of the words. The fact that words such as *sleeve*, *slide*, *slate* and *sleep* do not have such connotations proves that this is an open question.

The group can then experiment by making up their own *sl-* words and writing definitions for them. They may already be familiar with the example of *slithy* and its definition from Lewis Carroll's 'Jabberwocky' in *Alice through the Looking Glass* (1989, Dragon's World).

Further activity
Other examples of such letter patterns are the ending *-le*, which often suggests something small (*icicle*, *winkle*, *trickle*) and the double vowel *ee* which also implies smallness in some of its occurrences (*wee*, *teeny*, *peep*). Both of these examples have many exceptions.

12. Word webs (2)

Age range
Five to eleven.

Group size
Small groups or the whole class.

What you need
Writing materials.

Curriculum context
A quick writing game that can be related to concepts arising from current work in the class.

What to do
This game runs along similar lines to Activity 6, but this time the teacher selects a stimulus which is a recognisable free morpheme. For example, with younger children the word *day* might be selected, giving rise to the pattern below.

The teacher can plan a visual display of the resulting array of words in ways that draw attention to features like spelling changes caused by the bolting on of suffixes, or the way in which some words are hyphenated and some not.

13. Identifying morphemes

Age range
Seven to eleven.

Group size
Small groups.

What you need
Dictionaries, writing materials.

Curriculum context
A lesson-long activity based on the vocabulary of a given topic area.

What to do
Some units of meaning in English words are derived from other languages, notably Latin and Greek in the case of scientific vocabulary. Many of these root forms do not occur as independent words in English, though some of them are now entering the language in the guise of trade names and slang. For example, *bio*, given a capital letter, will be familiar to the children as the name of a type of yoghurt, *micro* is now in acceptable usage as the name of a type of computer, and *mega* is currently used as an expression of admiration.

Children can browse through dictionaries or information texts, collecting samples of words which contain such forms and speculating on the original meaning of the root form. Note that this can be an instructively hit-and-miss affair. Some words which appear to share roots, for instance, *illustrate* and *illness*, may originate from different sources, while the relationships between words which are related, such as *manipulate* and *manure*, may be too obscure for the children to grasp unassisted.

14. New words from old

Age range
Nine to eleven.

Group size
Small groups.

What you need
Word lists, writing materials.

Curriculum context
A lesson-long activity as part of a topic on word origins.

What to do
Provide the children with a list of words that share the same root and invite them to speculate on the meaning of the root. When a meaning has been agreed, encourage the children to check it in a dictionary. You can then show them how to incorporate this root into new made-up words by bolting on suffixes and prefixes, or isolating a morpheme that could not normally stand independently.

Original list: vivid, revive, survive, vivarium, convivial
New words: viv, subvive, vivian, devive, vivvier, megavivish

The group can then be invited to invent meanings for their new words, and to incorporate them into sentences from which other children can try to derive these meanings.

15. Morpheme shuffle

Age range
Nine to eleven.

Group size
Pairs.

What you need
Three sets of about twenty blank cards, each a different colour; felt-tipped pens.

Curriculum context
An oral game which might form part of a topic on word origins.

What to do
On one set of cards write out a set of common prefixes, on the second a set of common suffixes, and on the third a set of common root forms (see below for some suggestions). To start the game, each child takes half the cards from each set. They then take it in turns to lay out either a prefix with a root form, a root form with a suffix, or a root form sandwiched between a prefix and a suffix. Each child then has to invent a meaning for the new word created by the dealer.

Prefix	Root	Suffix
un	bio	able
sub	cycl	er
re	psych	ish
dis	therm	ise

Of course, it is possible that the children will come up with words already in the dictionary, in which case it would be interesting for them to compare their invented definitions with the official ones.

16. Antiscrabble

Age range
Children from seven to eleven who already have some confidence in spelling.

Group size
Two to four.

What you need
A Scrabble set (junior or adult).

Curriculum context
A word game, part of a topic on spelling or purely recreational. Curriculum applications are suggested in the 'Further activity' section.

What to do
The game is played in exactly the same way as conventional Scrabble, except for the following conditions:
• any words that can be found in the dictionary are disallowed;
• only words that can be pronounced are allowed;
• the player must offer a coherent definition for each word played.

The second condition ensures that random letter strings are disqualified.

This activity usually gives rise to interesting discussions on what letter strings are permissible in English.

Further activity
Children can collect their new words at the end of the game and practise writing dictionary definitions of them. These definitions might be based on the children's awareness of features such as morpheme patterns and onomatopoeia, and they can be related to a creative theme. For example, the words could be used as the basis for a Martian dictionary, or as the names of creatures in an imaginary bestiary which could then be annotated and illustrated.

17. Word processor

Age range
Five to eleven.

Group size
Any size, children working in pairs.

What you need
Writing materials.

Curriculum context
A quick handwriting activity that can be used to add a little variety to daily practice.

Investigating letter patterns

What to do
Ask the children to write any word that they are familiar with at the top of the page. They should then write out all possible *pronounceable* rearrangements of all the letters in the original word, as in the example below:

> *Computer*: terumpoc, putrecom, trepucom, pomcuter…

Each child in the pair should work individually and then compare their results.

Further activity
The results can be written up, illustrated, displayed and recited as examples of 'concrete poetry', perhaps using as inspiration Edwin Morgan's poem 'A Computer's First Christmas Card' in *Selected Poems* (1985, Carcanet).

18. Initial letters

Age range
Six to nine.

Group size
Small groups or pairs.

What you need
School documents (class and group lists, prospectuses, official letters, National Curriculum documents, and so on).

Curriculum context
A short reading/writing activity that could be part of a survey of environmental print.

What to do
Draw the children's attention to the fact that names can be represented by just their first letters, and that these letters are usually capitalised and sometimes followed by full stops. Encourage them to identify their own and other people's initials. Can they guess what unknown initials might stand for? What about initials like PE, RE, NC, and so on? Football teams, postcodes, atlases and product names are other sources. Can any be found in newspapers, magazines and notices around the school? The children or teacher can make lists of these initials and what they stand for. This can be followed by discussion of why people or organisations might prefer to be known by initials rather than full names.

19. Acronyms

Age range
Seven to eleven.

Group size
The whole class, working in pairs.

What you need
Writing materials.

Curriculum context
A quick writing game that could form part of a survey of environmental print.

What to do
Encourage the children to collect examples of acronyms from their reading and general knowledge, for example, UNESCO (**U**nited **N**ations **E**ducational, **S**cientific and **C**ultural **O**rganisation), laser (**l**ight **a**mplification by **s**timulated **e**mission of **r**adiation), radar (**ra**dio **d**etection **a**nd **r**anging). Can they make up their own acronyms which express a personal comment on some aspect of their lives? Show them how it might be done with the word 'books': **b**oring **'o**rrible **o**ld **k**nowledge **s**ources or **b**eautiful **o**bjects **o**ffering **k**nowledge and **s**kills.

Further activity
Draw the children's attention to ways in which the form of some acronyms reflects their meaning, for instance ASH (**A**ction on **S**moking and **H**ealth) or MADD (**M**others **A**gainst **D**runk **D**rivers). Encourage them to make up similar acronyms related to class concerns, such as **W**ildlife **A**rea **S**ite **P**rotection **S**quad.

20. Spoonerisms

Age range
Seven to eleven.

Group size
Small groups.

What you need
Writing materials, examples of historical and 'home-made' spoonerisms, a copy of *A Dormal Nay* from the Story Chest reading scheme (Nelson).

Curriculum context
A creative writing activity that can be offered during a writers' workshop session.

What to do
Explain to the children the origin and meaning of the term 'spoonerism'. The Reverend W.A. Spooner was a turn-of-the-century Oxford don who often transposed initial sounds in words. For example, he was said to have admonished a lazy student with the following words: 'Sir, you have tasted two whole worms; you have hissed all my mystery lectures and been caught fighting a liar in the quad; you will leave by the next town drain.'

Read from *A Dormal Nay*. This is a story about a day in the life of a schoolboy, but every sentence is peppered with spoonerisms, creating a highly humorous effect. Then invite the children to write their own poem, story, letter or description, using as many spoonerisms as they can.

You might also like to refer to Dick King-Smith's *The Hodgeheg* (1989, Puffin) in the course of this activity.

21. Alphabet sentences (pangrams)

Age range
Seven to eleven.

Group size
Small groups.

What you need
Dictionaries, writing materials.

Curriculum context
A writing game involving dictionary practice for children who are gaining some confidence in spelling.

What to do
The typists' practice sentence, *The quick brown fox jumps over the lazy dog* contains every letter in the alphabet, in a sequence of 35 letters. Challenge the children to write a similar, but even shorter, sentence. Some failed attempts at this task are illustrated.

As well as requiring close attention to the spellings of words, this activity encourages the children to explore uncommon words and sentence patterns, which have to be resorted to in order to produce compact sentences. This makes it a challenging activity for reasonably skilled and competent writers, but it should not be allowed to become a drudgerous plod for other children.

22. Shannon's game or Hangman

Age range
Five to seven.

Group size
Small groups or the whole class.

What you need
Shared writing materials.

Curriculum context
A spelling game that can be played at the start or end of the day, or between other lessons. It can support the learning of topic-related vocabulary, as well as increasing general awareness of the serial probability of letter sequences in English.

What to do
Think of a word that you want the children to pay particular attention to. For each letter in the word's spelling, mark a dash on the board or flipchart. Ask the children to guess the first letter. If they fail to do so within a reasonably short amount of time, supply the letter, as this game becomes boring if it is not kept brisk.

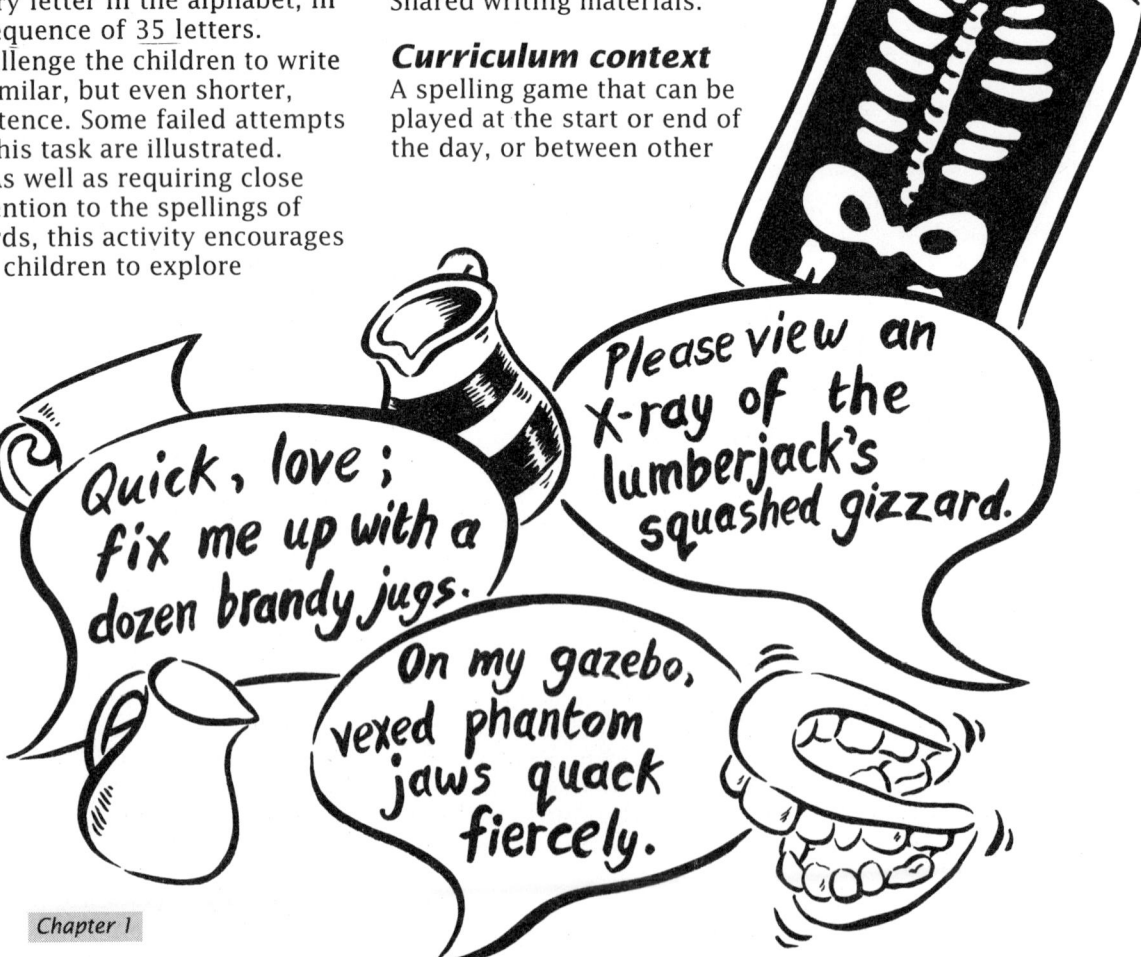

Quick, love; fix me up with a dozen brandy jugs.

Please view an X-ray of the lumberjack's squashed gizzard.

On my gazebo, vexed phantom jaws quack fiercely.

Once the first letter has been supplied, encourage the children to think about what is *likely* to come next. For example, if *t* is the first letter, *h* or *r* or any of the vowels are possible, but not *b*, *c*, *d*, *f* and so on. Continue this exploration until enough of the spelling has been uncovered for the children to identify the word.

Further activity
This is a game which the children can play in pairs once it has been learned in the whole-class context. It can be used to practise difficult spellings.

In the 'Hangman' variant, the children are invited to guess at any of the letters which might be in the word, the teacher slotting correct guesses into their proper positions. There is a greater likelihood that children will make random guesses in this game, but an opportunity is also provided for the teacher to encourage children to think about what letters might *precede* the letters already uncovered.

23. Skeleton writing

Age range
Nine to eleven.

Group size
Small groups, working in pairs.

What you need
Writing materials; examples of classified ads and other shortened forms of communication, such as telegrams, shopping lists and diary notes, where there is no real need to write everything out in full. These can be made up by the teacher.

Curriculum context
A short investigation of spelling patterns, vowels and consonants which could form part of a topic on codes.

What to do
Let the children examine the classified ads and other messages and ask them to try to reconstruct them in full. This should be relatively easy, since key features of the essential words will act as cues.

Now take the reconstructed messages and experiment with the effects of the following types of skeleton writing:
• leaving out all the consonants, rather than the vowels;
• providing just the first half of every word;
• providing just the second half;
• leaving out every other letter of the message;
• doing any of the above, but providing a dash or asterisk to mark each deletion.

Discuss why certain parts of words appear to be more informative than others. Children who are familiar with scripts such as Arabic and Hebrew, where vowels are not fully identified, might be able to provide an interesting perspective on this.

Investigating letter patterns

24. Playing with spelling possibilities

Age range
Nine to eleven.

Group size
Small groups, working in pairs.

What you need
Writing materials, a copy of the anonymous poem, 'Hints on Pronunciation for Foreigners' (photocopiable page 204).

Curriculum context
An investigation of letter patterns related to a topic on writing in advertising and the media. It is best suited to children already familiar with conventional spellings.

What to do
Give the children a list of words and, with reference to the ambiguities highlighted in 'Hints on Pronunciation for Foreigners', invite them to invent new spellings for these words. These spellings will of course be incorrect, but should conform to spelling patterns present in similarly pronounced words, for instance, 'today' could become *tooday*, *tudeigh* or *2day*.

Further activity
This type of playful spelling is frequently used by shops and other businesses, often in conjunction with puns and alliteration, to catch the attention of potential customers, for example, Kwiksave or Gatwick Hair-Port. Children will enjoy collecting such examples from the local environment and from the Yellow Pages, and then having a go at creating their own advertising slogans based on such word play.

25. The 'natural history' of individual letters

Age range
Five to eleven.

Group size
Small groups.

What you need
Writing materials, dictionaries.

Curriculum context
A small-scale investigation of the alphabet which could form part of a language awareness programme.

What to do
Allow each child or pair of children in the group to choose a favourite letter. Ask them to record all that they know about that particular letter. This can be done through talk, writing and drawing, and might include the following:
- the number of different ways the letter might be written;
- the number of different sounds it might represent;
- collections of words beginning or ending with the letter;
- abbreviations and acronyms in which the letter occurs;
- idiomatic usages of the letter, for example, *X-ray*, *D-day*, *I-beam*.

Provide resources for further study of the letter. These might include examples of other scripts in which the letter occurs or from which it originates, a word-processor with different fonts, and, for older children, an advanced dictionary providing detailed information about each letter.

The children's findings can then be written up as reports, forming a reading resource for other children.

26. Letter frequency and codes

Age range
Nine to eleven.

Group size
Pairs, working on individual documents.

What you need
Writing materials; photocopies, enlarged if possible, of as many different types of text as you can collect. Each sample should be approximately 100 words long.

Curriculum context
An extended investigation which could form part of a study of communications or integrate with statistical work in mathematics.

What to do
Show the children how to tally the letters in their sample and to make a bar chart showing their frequency. Compare this with other samples and make a visual representation of the overall frequency of each letter.

Introduce the children to the symbols used in Morse code and Braille if they are not already familiar with them. Explain the general method of symbolising letters without showing them the equivalent of any specific letter. Given what they have discovered about letter frequency, can the children work out the most sensible arrangement of Morse or Braille symbols to ascribe to each letter of the Roman alphabet? Let them compare their results with the actual systems in use.

Further activity
Ask the pairs of children to devise their own symbols for a secret code, using visual marks, body language, musical sounds and so on, taking into account their work on letter frequency. They should then try sending short messages in these codes.

Discuss the difficulties of working with a letter-by-letter code. What other useful units of language (such as whole words, phrases and sentences) might it be sensible to denote by single symbols? Make a list of these high utility words, phrases and sentences, for example, *Danger, May I have ..., How do I get to ...*

Explain how other systems of communication, such as British Sign Language, deal with this issue. You may find *The Cambridge Encyclopaedia of Language* by David Crystal (1987, CUP) a useful reference.

27. A history of spelling

Age range
Nine to eleven.

Group size
Small groups.

What you need
Examples of English texts from different historical periods.

Curriculum context
An in-depth investigation of the development of English spelling that could form part of a history topic.

What to do
Ask the children to browse through the documents. They could try to write modern translations of more obscure material or to translate contemporary material into the spelling patterns of an earlier age. Help the children to arrange the documents in a tentative time-line based on their similarities with modern English.

You could then discuss some of the following topics:
- evidence of greater flexibility in spelling before the time of widespread printing;
- evidence of changes in pronunciation;
- use of conventions that have died out in modern English (such as the use of *f* to represent the *s* sound in some positions) or have survived only in special cases such as the use of ¥ for *th* as in *¥e Olde Tea Shoppe*);
- different styles of calligraphy.

CHAPTER 2

Words and meanings

At first sight, the concept of a word seems quite straightforward; we are surrounded by them from birth. The number of words a six-year-old can understand has been estimated at 14,000, while the vocabulary of an educated adult can be anything from 50,000 to 250,000 words (Jean Aitchison, Words in the Mind, 1987, Blackwell).

Children rapidly gain all sorts of personal and cultural knowledge about words: they have favourite words and words they hate, and learn very quickly about taboo words and words that wound. They also discover the playful potential of words very early, enjoying the sounds of unfamiliar words and later appreciating the fluidity of meaning in many jokes and puns. This fascination with words persists for many people throughout their lives, and is seen in the popularity of media word games, word search and crossword books, and games like Scrabble and Pictionary.

However, what counts as a word? Should schoolchildren count as one or two words; are swim, swimming, swam and swum separate words or variants of the first term? Children will have to consider this question when working with dictionaries. What about idioms such as get on like a house on fire, where the words together add up to more than their individual meanings?

Meaning is itself an elusive quality. What a word means for you might not correspond with what it means for me. The variations will reflect our experiences of the concept denoted by the word, our attitudes towards it and perhaps even our individual aesthetic reactions to the sound of the word. It will also reflect the differences in social groups and the overall context within which the word is used. A child describing something as 'wicked' when talking to friends is unlikely to mean the same thing as a clergyman using the word in a sermon.

BACKGROUND

This particular example also illustrates the way in which word meanings alter over time, becoming broader or narrower in scope, and sometimes changing completely. This is often a matter of fashion, though sometimes it is in response to social or technological changes: consider the way in which familiar words like *friendly* (as in *user-friendly* and *ozone friendly*) and *mouse* have acquired new uses recently. Such changes will also bring entirely new words into the dictionary (for example, *droob*, *Majorism* and *pixel* from the 1993 edition of the *Shorter Oxford English Dictionary*, OUP) while bestowing the kiss of death upon others.

People often react to such changes by insisting that we shun all but the most essential new words and hold fast to the 'original' meanings of words already in use. In Shakespeare's time, writers like Edmund Spencer were attempting to resist the influx of neologisms (newly-coined terms), which were flooding into English as a result of the rediscovery of classical learning, the expansion of science and world exploration. Shakespeare himself, though one of the most prolific neologisers (we owe to him words like *assassination*, *barefaced*, *countless*, *courtship*, *dwindle* and *laughable*), nevertheless made fun of such ridiculous innovations as *remuneration* and *posterior*. About a hundred years after Shakespeare's death, Jonathan Swift was protesting against such crude terms as *sham*, *banter*, *bully* and *bamboozle*. A generation later Doctor Johnson was arguing against words like *clever*, *fun* and *stingy*, while nearer to our own time, Sir Earnest Gowers, in his influential *Complete Plain Words* (1962, Pelican), was warning against an invasion of *-ise* verbs such as *hospitalise* and *publicise*. The fact that all of these once objectionable terms have now become respectable parts of English vocabulary shows the futility of struggling too hard against neologisms.

The other half of the purist argument, that we should cling to the original meanings of the words we already have, is undermined by its own assumptions. If, for example, the 'correct' meaning of the word *nice* is *precise*, because that is what it meant in Shakespeare's time, could we not argue that *ignorant* is an even more correct meaning, since that is the meaning of

Grammar Parts of speech

the Latin word *nescius* from which *nice* is derived? The history of words is fascinating, but it does not provide any authority for the way in which they should be used.

This does not imply that 'anything goes' in the use of words, and that we should accept language change unthinkingly. Phenomena like the use of a word in a new context, a subtle change in word meaning, the invention of a new word, or the retention of an old word beyond its sell-by date can have either creative or destructive effects. Some neologisms and shifts of usage are conscious attempts to disguise ugly truths (for example, the recent use of the term *ethnic cleansing*). The perseverance of outmoded usages can also have bad effects: many terms that were once uncontroversial now have sexist and racist connotations.

Given the importance of words, what do children need to be taught about them? Traditional grammar divided words up into eight parts of speech. These are listed below, together with their traditional definitions.
- nouns – 'naming words' (*cat, hailstone, truth*);
- pronouns – words that 'stand for' nouns (*it, he, they*);
- adjectives – words that describe nouns (*green, three, stupid*);
- verbs – 'doing words' (*run, hope, leave*);
- adverbs – words that qualify verbs, adjectives, phrases and sentences (*very, sluggishly, soon*);
- prepositions – words that indicate how nouns are related in space or time (*on, in, after*);
- conjunctions – words that join up other elements in a sentence (*and, so, but*);
- interjections – exclamations (*oh, oops, alas*).

There are several problems associated with this way of classifying words, especially the vagueness of the criteria for allocating words to a particular category. If a verb is defined as a 'doing word', imagine a child's response when asked to identify the verb in a sentence like *The team needed six more runs to win*. If pronouns 'stand for' nouns, what does *it* stand for in a sentence like *It's raining*? Does the use of a preposition in a phrase like *in spite of* really have anything to do with a spatial relationship? The adverb category is so loosely defined that it includes words of widely diverse functions (*tomorrow, when, not, too, ridiculously*). The amount of effort spent teaching children to allocate words to these rather suspect categories has helped give traditional grammar such a bad name. It is not just the shakiness of the classification that is regrettable, but the fact that an emphasis on classification diverts attention away from considerations of what words can actually do.

This is not to say that we can do without terminology altogether. If we are to encourage children to discuss words, we need a language in which to hold that discussion, and traditional terms like the names of the parts of speech will form a useful part of that language. Accordingly, several of the activities in this chapter provide opportunities for the use of these terms.

The activities in this chapter cover the broad areas of functions, connotations and meaning change, encouraging children to consider the origins, uses, effects of and relationships between words. Underlying the activities is an acknowledgement that children already have a wealth of knowledge about words, and the hope that by reflecting on this knowledge they will become more aware of the manipulative and creative power of language.

ACTIVITIES

1. Names and name origins

Age range
Five to seven.

Group size
The whole class, working in groups of four to six.

What you need
Writing and art materials; a book on name meanings, such as L. Dunkling and W. Gosling's *Dictionary of First Names* (1983, Dent).

Curriculum context
An activity suitable for the beginning of the school year with a new reception class, to help the children get to know each other. It could also be used as part of a topic on names and name origins with older children.

What to do
Before you introduce this activity, prepare a poster or a 'big book' with information in large, bold print on the origins of the first names of all the children in your class.

Explain to the children that every personal name has a story behind it, and illustrate this fact by giving examples from the *Dictionary of First Names*.

Now ask the children to write out their own first names (you may need to help younger children to do this) and encourage them to discuss what they might mean. When they have had a go at inventing a meaning or origin, display the poster or big book, so that the children can compare their own ideas with the actual origin.

This activity provides opportunities to discuss naming traditions in other cultures and to look for foreign equivalents for English names. Bilingual children who can write their names in one or more different scripts can be encouraged to share this skill with the other children.

50 Chapter 2

2. Researching place names

Age range
Five to eleven.

Group size
The whole class or a small group.

What you need
Maps and atlases, books with information on the origins of local place names, writing and display materials.

Curriculum context
A topic on local history that could be adapted to a more distant geographical area.

What to do
Ask the children to study the maps and make lists of all the different place names that they can see. Ask them to think of how they might categorise these names. In a local history topic the following categories might emerge:
• names of towns and villages;
• names of parks, woods, rivers and other non-residential areas;
• names of housing estates, blocks of flats and farms;
• names of streets;
• names of hospitals, prisons, schools and other institutions;

In a topic covering a wider geographical area, the categories might include countries and counties, lakes, seas and mountain ranges.

Having compiled these lists, the children can then be encouraged to discuss any of the following themes:
• the meanings and origins of the place names (you should provide appropriate reference material);
• regularities in the structure of the place names, for example, the common English suffixes *-don* and *-caster*, the Welsh prefix *Llan-* and the Irish and West Country *Kil-*. This can be related to any work on morphemes that the children might have done (see Chapter 1);
• the history of the place name. You could provide reference material about the circumstances involved in any change of name, and encourage the children to think about who actually decides what a place should be called.

Further activity
In the case of a local study, the children can rename any places that they think they can invent a better name for. This could be organised as a school or class game involving an opinion survey on new names, followed by a referendum.

3. Inventing place names

Age range
Five to eleven.

Group size
Small groups.

What you need
Writing and art materials.

Curriculum context
A prelude or illustration to a storytelling activity, or any topic involving making or reading maps.

What to do
For younger children, provide a map of an imaginary island, town or other type of area for each child. Geographical features should be marked in but not place names. Older children who have had more experience with map-making should be able to create such a map themselves.

Encourage the children to talk about where the place on the map might be and what things might be like there. Stress that as the place is purely imaginary, their ideas can be as outrageous as they like. Modelling the process with a map of your own, get the children to invent place names, using their knowledge of the factors and conventions underlying the place names they already know. They can then annotate their maps with explanations of their chosen names.

With younger children, this can be done as a shared writing activity centred on a big map of a place which the children have visited in a story; for example, the land of Maurice Sendak's *Where the Wild Things Are* (1967, Bodley Head). The children should discuss possibilities for place names and the teacher can write them on the map after the decisions have been made.

Further activity
The place names of the seas and mountain ranges of the moon can be used to introduce children to Latin in a fascinating and poetic context. A topic on astronomy could also bring in the names of the planets and their origins

4. Renaming

Age range
Five to seven.

Group size
A small group or the whole class.

What you need
Shared writing materials.

Curriculum context
A short talking and writing game that could arise from the description of an imaginary place or form part of the language work in any topic.

What to do
Ask the children how they think days of the week (or months of the year) acquired their names. If the children's response is pure perplexity, you will have some storytelling to do. *The Oxford Dictionary of English Etymology* (1966, OUP) is the most authoritative source for this information, but the basic facts are:
- Sunday – day of the sun
- Monday – day of the moon
- Tuesday – Tiu's day
- Wednesday – Woden's day
- Thursday – Thor's day
- Friday – Freya's day
- Saturday – Saturn's day

The discovery that names are *given* to things, rather than being a natural attribute like shape or colour, is a significant one for children.

Now, selecting stimuli that fit in with a current topic or story, invite the children to invent new names. Encourage them to reproduce the pattern of conventional names. For example, what new morpheme (or 'word bit') might we use instead of *-day* if we are renaming the days of the week? Does it have to come at the end of the word?

Encourage the children to think about appropriate-sounding words (introducing the concept of onomatopoeia) and words that reflect a resemblance between the thing to be named and something else (introducing the concept of metaphor). The giant's vocabulary in Roald Dahl's *BFG* (1982, Jonathan Cape) should provide some entertaining models for this activity. The children could also consider the following example:

In the Land of Three there are only three days: *Gogbustle*, when everybody does their working and shopping, *Gogmunch*, when everybody gets together to eat, and *Gogsnorgle*, the day in between when everybody sleeps...

Further activity
With older children, you can play at inventing words for things which do not appear to have any names, such as the following:
• the feeling of anticipation which precedes a sneeze;
• the tendency of random marks suddenly to form meaningful patterns.

5. Inventing names for characters

Age range
Five to eleven.

Group size
A small group.

What you need
Photographs of people cut out of newspapers or magazines.

Curriculum context
A quick word game that can be used as a prelude to story writing.

What to do
Talk to the children about their favourite book characters, share your own and make a list of any of those whose names seem to reflect something about their characters. Again, Roald Dahl is a good source for such names (Willy Wonka, Mr Twit, Miss Trunchbull) as is Charles Dickens. You could discuss with the children what it might be about some sounds that suggests particular qualities. You could refer to any work on onomatopoeia that the children may have done (see pages 35–36 in Chapter 1).

Show the children the pictures and, after discussing what kind of personalities the people in the pictures might have, ask them to devise appropriate names and to explain why they have chosen these names.

6. Business names

Age range
Six to eleven.

Group size
Small groups.

What you need
Writing materials; photocopied entries from Yellow Pages, local directories or advertisements from local newspapers.

Curriculum context
A survey related to a topic on advertising or the local environment, that can be extended into creative writing.

What to do
Show the children the names of local businesses that use language play to attract the customer's attention. Ask the children if they can identify the type of business from the name alone. What, for example, do *Timbercure*, *Chestnut Landscapes* and *Blueflash Movers* do?

Help the children to identify the kind of language play that each name is using. They could then try to invent similar

7. Dinosaur names

Age range
Six to nine.

Group size
Small groups or the whole class.

What you need
Art materials, pictures of dinosaurs, a large chart showing the Greek derivations of the names of dinosaurs (see photocopiable page 205).

Curriculum context
A lesson-long activity that can be related to a topic on dinosaurs, animal names or word study.

What to do
Show the children the dinosaur pictures and the chart of name origins, and explain how the dinosaurs' names derive from their physical features. The children can then design their own dinosaurs, inventing suitable names by combining the morphemes on the chart.

The teacher can introduce the children to the Latin names of plants and animals through examples such as the harebell (*campanula rotundiflora*: bell with round leaves).

8. Keywords

Age range
Five to seven.

Group size
Individuals.

What you need
A set of blank cards, writing and drawing materials.

Curriculum context
These activities can be used in the early stages of reading instruction to interest children

names for a variety of businesses. A variant of this activity that older children find amusing is to devise names that subvert the intentions of the advertiser, for instance, *Renchall and Redspit, the Gentle Dentists* or *Sir Kit Short, Electrical Consultant*.

Words and meanings

in words. With older children they can be used to extend knowledge about the relationships between words.

What to do

This activity is based on the Keywords strategy described by Sylvia Ashton Warner in *Teacher* (1963, Simon & Schuster). Ask each child which word he or she wants to learn, then write the word on a blank card. The child can then trace, copy and illustrate the chosen word, keeping the card in his or her possession. Help the child to build up a deck of keywords and go through them regularly together. Ashton Warner suggests that if the child cannot read the word after one look, it should be removed from the deck.

Words from the deck can be used for a variety of talking and writing activities:
• Select one of the words from the deck and encourage the child to free associate from it, writing new words down as the child produces them. The child can then free associate from the new words, producing a chain reaction that can continue *ad infinitum*.
• Show how rhyming and alliterative words can be produced and help the child write out any rhymes and sentences created through this process, so that they can be illustrated and collected.
• Select appropriate words as starting points for the spelling and handwriting letter string activities outlined in the previous chapter.
• When the child is confident about reading and writing an individual word use that word to show the child the patterns which relate it to similar words.

Similar activities can be used with confident readers and writers to explore more sophisticated aspects of word structure:
• Ask the child to select a word and write out all the variants related to it. Supply any that you know of that the child may not, for example, *run, ran, runs, running, runner, rerun, runny, runway*.
Now, help the child to identify which of these forms is the one used as the headword in dictionaries. (It will not necessarily be the one that has been written out as a keyword.)
• Select a keyword and explore through word webbing its associations with other words. These can be associations of sound, such as rhyme, alliteration and assonance (vowel-rhyme, as in *fight* and *glide*), synonymy (similarity of meaning, such as *horse* and *steed*), antonymy (opposition of meaning, such as *exciting* and *boring*) and collocation (a much looser 'belonging together' of words, such as *fish* with *shark, fin, sea* and *chips*).
• Help the children to use dictionaries and other reference material to trace the history of the word.

9. Personal words (favourite and least favourite)

Age range
Five to eleven.

Group size
The whole class, then a small group.

What you need
Questionnaire format.

Curriculum context
A discussion activity that can follow any discussion of vocabulary. The survey can form part of a topic on 'Ourselves'.

What to do
Talk to the class about favourite and least favourite words. Tell the children about your own and try to explain what it is about certain words that you like or dislike. Encourage the children to do the same. The reasons why people like or dislike certain words can be very difficult to express, but the following categories may be helpful:
• words that people find difficult to dissociate from the things that they represent: *I hate the word 'sick' because every time I hear it I feel sick.*
• words attached to some personal experience: *I hate the word 'ambulance' because my cat got squashed by one.*
• words which are liked or disliked because of their sound: *I don't know what 'combustion' means but when I say it it makes me think of a big table covered in lovely food.*

Help the children to design a questionnaire and to conduct a survey of favourite and least favourite words throughout the school and at home. They can then compare the words provided by different age groups and genders.

10. Choosing adjectives (1)

Age range
Five to seven.

Group size
Small groups.

What you need
Any objects related to the current class topic, shared writing materials.

Curriculum context
Shared writing, preferably topic-related so that the activity supports other relevant activities.

What to do
Let the children examine the object by touch (using a 'feely box' if appropriate), visually (with and without a lens) and by smell. Discuss their contributions and write down the children's descriptive words and phrases on a chart with columns for texture, shape, size, colour and so on.

Ask the children if they can think of other objects and situations that selected words and phrases could be applied to. Charts can then be made to show how these words can have metaphorical as well as literal applications.

Words and meanings

11. Choosing adjectives (2)

Age range
Six to eleven.

Group size
Small groups.

What you need
Any visual media (newspaper or magazine picture, advertisement, video clip) or audio material (tape of a voice, environmental noise, music).

Curriculum context
A survey in media education or in any cross-curricular topic.

What to do
Each group should choose a stimulus item and each member of the group write down descriptive words suggested by the stimulus. All the members of the group then share and discuss their responses.

Using the same stimulus, the group can then conduct a class survey which can be extended to other age groups and to teachers, parents and helpers. Some points to consider are:
• Are different adjectives used by different age groups?
• Do boys and girls use different adjectives?
• How do people explain or justify their choice of adjectives?

12. Descriptive word scrapbooks

Age range
Five to seven.

Group size
Individuals contributing to a class resource.

What you need
A3 sugar paper and boards, hole-punched and fitted with cords to make an A3 loose-leaf binder; felt-tipped pens; two or three pictures for each adjective, cut out of magazines or created yourself.

Curriculum context
An open-ended activity that children can contribute to on an *ad hoc* basis.

What to do
Explain to the children that they are going to build up a resource that will help them in their writing. Show them the folder, and on each page write a different adjective relevant to a topic that is being followed by the class. Disassemble the folder, give the children the pictures and ask them to match them to the appropriate page before sticking them in.

After this group activity, the folder should be reassembled and the children invited to draw or collect their own pictures to add to the scrapbook.

Further activity
The activity can be extended to develop the children's awareness of adverbs. You could start by making collections of action pictures, and later on challenge the children to collect illustrations for such terms as *slowly, lazily* and *gradually*. Once this challenge has been met, you can do the same for more difficult terms like *unfairly, unfortunately* and *suddenly*.

13. Adjective riddles

Age range
Five to eight.

Group size
Small groups or the whole class.

What you need
A set of cards, each with a noun related to the topic on one side and adjectives related to the noun on the other; several sets of blank cards.

Curriculum context
A topic-related reading and reasoning game that older children can prepare for younger classes.

What to do
Spread the cards out in front of the children with the adjectives showing but not the nouns. Explain that the children are to guess the words on the other side of the card. When they have had a few goes at doing this, show them how to write their own card on a particular theme. Suitable cards for a topic on 'Weather' are shown in the table.

The children can then observe younger children who are following the topic playing their game in order to check its difficulty level. See Chapter 3, page 85 for a more sophisticated version of this game.

Side one	Side two
warm bright pleasant	sunlight
high thin feathery	cirrus
bright sudden dangerous	lightning
windy violent destructive	hurricane
cold hard slippery	ice

14. Soluble fish

Age range
Six to eleven.

Group size
A small group or the whole class.

Curriculum context
A poetry-writing game. The early stages can be played as an oral game.

What to do
Sit the children in a circle and nominate one of them to name an adjective describing something in the children's field of vision. The next person has to provide the noun to go with that adjective, and then to name an adjective for the next person.

Words and meanings

The game develops into 'soluble fish', a phrase coined by the surrealist leader André Breton, when the children deliberately join adjectives to inappropriate nouns to make bizarre phrases. The teacher can supply nouns and adjectives (and 'adjectival nouns') on cards and ask the children to make interesting juxtapositions. This may result in such odd phrases as *liquid skeleton, chocolate kettle, iron candle, skinless balloon* and *blazing snowman*, which can then be used as starting points for poems, stories, songs, slogans and sayings:

> Fructiloam Ultra Compost – rich enough to make an iceberg fertile!

Further activity
Children may appreciate the term *oxymoron* – linking normally incompatible words for rhetorical effect. Some well-known examples are *Parting is such sweet sorrow; a living death; dreadfully good.*

15. Collective nouns

Age range
Seven to eleven.

Group size
A small group or the whole class.

What you need
A list of collective nouns for your own reference (Eric Partridge's *Usage and Abusage* (1973, Penguin) contains an interesting list of actual and fanciful collectives), pictures to illustrate these nouns, writing materials.

Curriculum context
A writing game to start the day off or to fill in time before a break. It could also be used to explore the vocabulary of a specific topic or subject area.

What to do
Show the children the illustrated examples of collective nouns and ask them to add any that they know themselves. Explain that in many cases there is no accepted term for a collection of particular objects and that it is their job to invent such terms. For instance *a clog of parked cars* or *a rust of autumn leaves*.

You can also use the activity as part of the children's work in topic or subject areas: A topic on 'Nature' may produce *a galaxy of frogspawn, a pepperpot of spores*, and *a treasury of pollen grains.*

16. Insults

Age range
Seven to eleven.

Group size
The whole class.

What you need
A list of obscure insults (see photocopiable page 206), writing materials, dictionaries.

Curriculum context
A recreational activity to arouse children's curiosity about peculiarities of language. It can also be related

How dare you call me a doddypoll you scoddy fustilugs

to the more serious issue of playground name-calling.

What to do
Show the children the word chart and ask them to guess what the words have in common. If they cannot make the connection, define a couple of the words for them (all the definitions can be found in either the *Oxford English Dictonary* or in Chambers) and explain that they are largely obsolete terms of insult. The children can then discuss the sounds of the words and try to work out their meanings, later checking their definitions against the ones in the dictionaries. Because all of these terms are either rare or obsolete, this may be an opportunity to discuss how and why words fall out of use.

17. Core vocabulary

Age range
Seven to eleven.

Group size
Small groups.

What you need
Writing materials.

Curriculum context
A drama and discussion activity that can be used as a prelude to a creative writing project or an opinion survey on attitudes towards various topics.

What to do
Ask the children, in their groups, to imagine any of the following situations:
- they have been stranded in a country and know nothing of the language;
- they have landed on a distant planet and realise that it is inhabited;
- they have suddenly lost their power of speech.

Now ask them to identify which ten or twenty words they would most need to communicate, and to devise ways of achieving such

Words and meanings

communication. When they have done this, discuss the following points with them:
- reasons behind differences of opinion as to what the core words should be;
- the different amount of difficulty involved in communicating each word (this could lead to a discussion of concrete and abstract terms);
- the relative merits of communication through speech, movement, writing or drawing;
- which of the words represent things or ideas, which actions and which qualities (a context for using the terms *noun, verb, adjective* and so on);

The children could conclude by producing a phrase book based on their core vocabulary, showing in diagrammatic form the types of gesture or graphics that they have devised.

Further activity
The idea of 'most important words' can be extended to other areas as an indicator of people's attitudes. As part of a topic on homes or jobs, a group of children could conduct a survey to find out what ten words occur most immediately to people when they are asked to think about a given environment. The subjects could then be asked to try to explain why those words occurred to them.

This activity can be related to the activity on Reduced language in Chapter 6, page 188.

18. Words and places

Age range
Seven to eleven.

Group size
The whole class.

What you need
Writing materials, pictures or a video of a particular environment.

Curriculum context
A descriptive writing activity to introduce and organise the terminology of a new topic.

What to do
This activity is based on Sandy Brownjohn's 'Places and Details' (*What Rhymes With Secret?* 1982, Hodder and Stoughton). Ask the children to observe or imagine an environment related to the topic they are to study: pictures or a video will help. After the observation time, ask the children to name as many things as they can which they are likely to see in this environment and write their suggestions on the board or flip chart. You can then ask for

19. Adverbs: sports commentary

Age range
Seven to eleven.

Group size
The whole class, then small groups.

What you need
Tape recorder, recordings of sports commentaries.

Curriculum context
Oral composition based on PE which can be extended to any topic being followed by the class.

What to do
Play the recordings of the sports commentaries to the children and ask them to list all the adverbs that are used. Encourage them to reflect on the descriptive function of these words by considering what the commentary would sound like without them.

Then let the children compose a commentary for themselves. A 'first draft' could be recorded as a live commentary on an actual game being played at school or watched on the television with the sound turned down. It could then be listened to and redrafted in the light of discussion.

Further activity
This type of composition could be extended to observations of other stimuli, for example:
- nursery children in a play area;
- a video of traffic at a busy road junction;
- action scenes from wildlife films.

20. Adverb poem

Age range
Six to eleven.

Group size
The whole class.

words and phrases which describe these things or the environment as a whole, writing them down alongside the first list.

The children should then choose any items from the first list and describe them in one or two lines, using any appropriate vocabulary which has been suggested. (This activity provides an opportunity to introduce older children to terms like *noun*, *verb*, *adjective* and *adjectival phrase*.)

Words and meanings

What you need
Writing materials.

Curriculum context
Poetry writing arising from the preceding activity.

What to do
Give the children a set of adverbs produced during the previous activity. Ask them to use these adverbs as the first word of each line of a poem. The poem might relate to the original stimulus or it might be about another subject of the children's own choosing.

The children can then discuss the differences between the oral and written compositions. They could also discuss the effect of shifting the adverb from the beginning of the sentence ('front focusing') to its more normal position immediately before or after the verb.

21. Preposition poems

Age range
Seven to eleven.

Group size
Small groups.

What you need
Writing materials.

Curriculum context
Poetry writing.

What to do
This activity is described in Sandy Brownjohn's *Does It Have to Rhyme?* (1980, Hodder and Stoughton). The group decide on a theme that they want to write about. Each child is assigned a different preposition and writes one line beginning with that preposition. Then the children decide on an order for their lines and write out the resulting poem.

Alternatively, having chosen a theme, children can work

individually, writing a poem where every line starts with a different preposition:

The Wildlife Garden
Under the rocks the woodlice snuggle.
Over the pond the pond skaters skim.
Amongst the leaves the hedgehog hides.
In the soil the roots search slowly.

22. Idiomatic prepositions

Age range
Six to eleven.

Group size
The whole class.

What you need
Writing materials.

Curriculum context
An oral or written activity that could form part of a language awareness topic.

What to do
Explain that many phrases for describing how people feel use prepositions in a metaphorical way. Show the children a list of such phrases and see how many are familiar to them, for example:

At sixes and sevens
Down in the dumps
In the dog house
Under the weather
Over the moon
On my nerves
Beside herself

Ask the children for any that they know themselves and add them to the list. Discuss how these sayings might have originated and compare their meanings with the literal uses of prepositions. *Bears in the Night* by S. and J. Berenstain (1981, Collins) would be a useful resource here.

Encourage the children to invent some of their own phrases and slot them into sentences. Other children can then try to guess the meanings of the new phrases from these sentences. For instance,

She's been *over the rainbow* since she got back from her holidays.

Don't eat that: it'll make you feel *under the slug*.

23. Jokes: homonymy and polysemy

Age range
Five to eleven.

Group size
The whole class.

Words and meanings 65

What you need
Joke books, writing and display materials.

Curriculum context
An open-ended anthologising activity intended to raise children's awareness of relationships between words.

What to do
Encourage the children to share any jokes they know. These can be written out, illustrated and collected to make a classroom joke book.

Ask the children to try to explain the humorous impact of their jokes and to identify those that work through word play. These can then be sorted into various categories:
• effects based on playing with word class:

How do you make a Swiss roll?
Push him off an Alp.

(compound noun interpreted as noun followed by verb);

• effects based on homophony (similarity of sound between unrelated words):

What do you call a man with a spade in his head?
Doug.

An extension of this joke provides an opportunity to discuss morphology:

What to do you call a man without a spade in his head?
Douglas.

(syllable *-las* interpreted as suffix *-less*);
• effects based on polysemy (the same word having different meanings):

What did the big chimney say to the little chimney?
You're too young to smoke.

Once familiar with these categories, the children can then browse through the published books to find further examples, although it may be difficult to persuade them to do so from a purely grammatical point of view.

24. Kennings

Age range
Seven to nine.

Group size
The whole class.

What you need
Examples of 'kennings' as given opposite.

66 Chapter 2

Idea	Anglo-Saxon kenning	Your kenning
body	bone house	
river	swan lane	
sword	battle torch	
sea	whale path	
sky	hawk field	
ship	sea plough	

Curriculum context
A creative writing activity that could be an inspiration for poetry writing. It could also form part of a topic on English history and literature, perhaps after reading a translation of Beowulf.

What to do
Explain that 'kennings' are vivid phrases from Anglo-Saxon literature, coined by poets as metaphors for common words. Then give the children a selection of kennings and ask them what they think these phrases might refer to before showing them the actual 'translations'.

Read the children some poetry or poetic descriptions using kennings (you should try writing this for yourself to get a feel for the activity), and invite them to interpret the phrases you have invented. The children can then try inventing kennings of their own using the format above. Having practised this descriptive device they can go on to use it in their poetic writing.

25. Euphemisms

Age range
Seven to eleven.

Group size
Small groups.

What you need
Examples of euphemisms from literature, people's speech and the media; newspapers and magazines.

Curriculum context
Media studies.

What to do
Give the children one of the two lists below. The first is a set of historical terms for the noun *toilet*, the second a list of more recent terms for the verb *to kill*. Ask the children to work out what single term the words might refer to.

List one
wardrobe
jakes
outhouse
privy
water closet

List two
neutralise
take out
terminate
liquidate
put to sleep

When this has been done, introduce the term *euphemism*, and discuss why this phenomenon occurs. You should mention that although euphemism is often used to mislead, it might also be used in a considerate manner to spare people's feelings. You could then ask the children to collect examples of euphemisms from the newspapers and magazines, and discuss whether they are being used considerately, dishonestly or just unthinkingly. Some recent euphemisms are:

let go – sack
incident – crime, atrocity...
standard class – lower class
client – patient, prisoner...

26. Meaning change: adjectives

Age range
Nine to eleven.

Group size
The whole class, then a small group.

What you need
Extracts from books and other texts which show changes in the use of adjectives over time. Two references are G. Hughes' *Words in Time – a social history of the English Vocabulary* (1988, Blackwell) and David Crystal's *Cambridge Encyclopaedia of Language* (1987, CUP).

27. Word changes

Curriculum context
A survey in English, suitable for a group of independent readers and writers, though the initial stage should be of interest to the whole class.

What to do
Start by talking to the whole class about what words they currently use as expressions of admiration (such words change with bewildering rapidity so no examples will be given). Tell the class about equivalent terms used when you were their age.

A smaller group can then use the textual material to research examples of changing usage. For example, relatively recent changes such as the trivialisation of words like *wicked* and *awesome* can be compared with long-term changes such as the shift in meaning of words like *silly* and *sophisticated*.

Age range
Seven to eleven.

Group size
A small group reporting to the whole class.

What you need
Copies of a questionnaire form; history books with illustrations of obsolete objects and practices; up-to-date catalogues of consumer goods; old and modern children's comics; newspapers from a generation or more ago ('day of birth' newspapers are a good resource here).

Curriculum context
An extended survey that could form part of a history project.

What to do
Let the children browse through the archival material, noting words which they think might fall into either of these two categories:

68 Chapter 2

ACID
(traditional): A corrosive liquid
(1960s): A hallucinogenic drug
(1990s): A style of music

MOUSE
(traditional): a small rodent
(1980s): an item of computer equipment

- words which were in use before they were born and have now become obsolete;
- words which were not in use before they were born and have now become common.

They can then attempt to work out meanings for any unfamiliar words.

Follow this up with a survey, giving questionnaire forms to parents, grandparents and other older people to gather data from as broad a stretch of time as possible. When all the information has been collected, the children can sort old and new words into nouns, verbs and adjectives which might reflect changes in available objects, changes in practices and changes in the way people describe things.

In all the categories, particularly the latter, there may be instances where obsolete words belong to a local dialect which is losing ground to standard English or to another, more vigorous local dialect. This provides an opportunity to discuss other factors in language change.

28. Predicting meaning change and stability

Age range
Nine to eleven.

Group size
Small groups.

What you need
A set of word cards showing how the meanings of some words have changed or been extended in recent memory (see illustration); writing materials; dictionaries.

Curriculum context
A creative examination of language change that also involves familiarisation with dictionary layout.

What to do
Refer back to previous activities on language change. Remind the children that such change is a continuous process and that many of the words we use now are likely to change their meanings, or acquire additional meanings, as time goes by.

Give the children the cards and ask them to discuss what meanings a specific word might acquire in the future. Choose one of their ideas and show, with the help of the dictionary, how definitions should be set out. (Depending on the previous experience of the children, you may need to explain the parts of speech terminology, and show how changes in spelling patterns might be involved in deriving adjectives from nouns or adverbs from adjectives). Let the children write out such definitions for themselves.

Further activity
Older children can be introduced to the distinction between content and function words by discussing which words from a given set (*and, acid, beauty, but, fish, if, is, mother*, for example) are most likely to maintain stable meanings. Function words are a small number of high frequency words such as articles, conjunctions and auxiliaries which indicate grammatical relationship in a

sentence but do not carry any independent meaning. Content words are a much larger class of lower frequency words, such as nouns, verbs and adjectives which do have independent meaning. In the sentence 'Hugo walked to the shops because of the bus strike' the function words are *to*, *the*, *because* and *of*. The rest are content words.

29. Babyword survey

Age range
Nine to eleven.

Group size
Small groups.

What you need
Tapes of the speech of preschool children.

Curriculum context
A topic on human development.

What to do
Encourage the children to reflect on what their first words were, and how their speech has changed as they have grown older. Parents can be interviewed to provide evidence of first words and phrases, and children with younger siblings can record their speech and make transcripts of carefully selected extracts. Discussion of this data might focus on any of the following areas:
• how to write down utterances that are not recognisable as words;
• similarities and differences in the early words of the children;
• what these early words might actually be referring to: objects, people, actions or feelings (the person who made the tape would have to provide some information about the context in which the speech occurred);
• what longer messages the child might be trying to convey through one- or two-word utterances. For example, how many different ways are there of interpreting an expression like 'Daddy bike': for instance, *that's Daddy's bike; Daddy's on a bike?*

30. Eponyms

Age range
Seven to nine.

Group size
Small groups.

What you need
List or dictionary of eponyms, such as *A Dictionary of Eponyms*, edited by Martin Manser (1988, Sphere).

Curriculum context
A short investigation of an aspect of English vocabulary. It could follow on from a topic in which such terms have been introduced. For example, a topic on electricity might involve the terms *amp*, *ohm* and *volt*.

What to do
Introduce the children to the idea of eponymy (using people's names as everyday words) either through terms

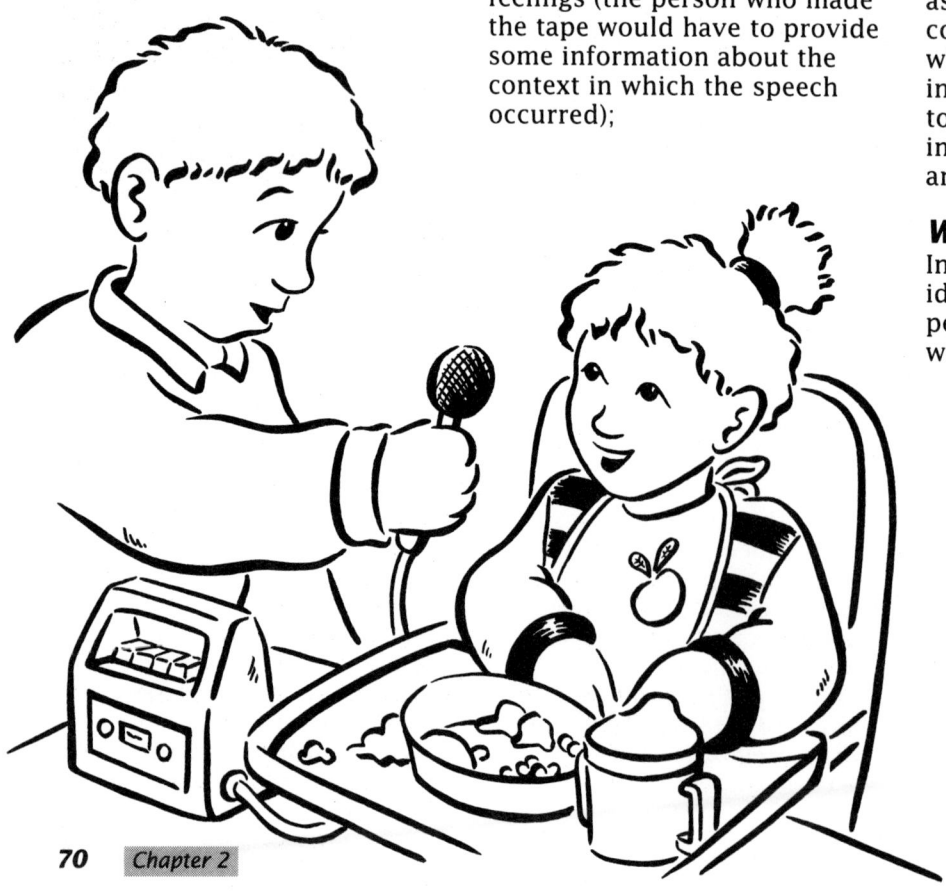

they have come across in topic work, or through such familiar examples as *wellington* and *sandwich*. You might note that though most eponymous terms are nouns, verb forms do occur occasionally, *bowdlerise* and *boycott* being two common examples.

Invite the children to write definitions of invented eponyms based on the names of people they know, using well-known habits or episodes as the basis of these coinages. A variation on this is to choose some present day celebrities and suggest definitions for eponymous nouns, verbs or adjectives based on their names. For instance,

The police moved in and made an *eastwood* of the whole gang.

The band decided to *geldoff* the profits from their latest album.

The children may also enjoy writing derivation for pseudo-eponyms – words that are not in fact eponymous. For example:

Farce *noun*: a ridiculous set of occurrences; a humourous play based on such occurrences.

This word is named after Sir Henry Farce, the last owner of the Happy Theatre. He was a miser and refused to maintain the building properly so it became infested with woodworm. One night, during the sword fight scene in Macbeth *the stage collapsed bringing the entire theatre down with it.*

Further activity
Investigate whether eponymy is a purely English phenomenon. Children who speak languages other than English can be asked to find out eponymous terms in these languages which can then be compared with terms in English. One point of comparison may be the gender of the eponyms. In English, the vast majority of these are male. Some exceptions are *curie*, *melba* and *Xanthippe*, the latter a derogatory term. Discuss with the children why this should be the case.

31. Playground game vocabulary

Age range
Seven to eleven.

Group size
Small groups.

What you need
A copy of *Children's Games in Street and Playground* by Iona and Peter Opie (1967, OUP); reference material about similar games from around the world, such as *Songs, Games and Stories from around the World* (a cassette and booklet produced by WORLDAWARE, The Centre for World Development Education); writing materials.

Curriculum context
A research project related to PE, a topic on games around the world or a topic on language diversity.

What to do
Ask the children to describe any games that they play at school or at home, explaining any specialised vocabulary that is used. (The traditional street games described by the Opies are probably in decline in many urban areas, but computer games should provide a rich source of such vocabulary.) Show them selected material from the Opies' book and from the books about children's games around the world. If possible, let the children try out some of these games.

After this preparatory exploration, groups of children can attempt to devise their own outdoor games based on the traditional models. Encourage them to invent their own vocabulary for 'peace terms', special actions, roles and so on. Russell Hoban and Quentin Blake's *How Tom Beat Captain Najork and His Hired Sportsmen* (1993, Random House) might provide an effective inspiration for this activity.

32. He words and she words (1)

Age range
Nine to eleven.

Group size
Small groups.

33. He words and she words (2)

What you need
A range of everyday reading matter: comics, magazines, newspapers, direct mail advertisements, catalogues. A chart for displaying results.

Curriculum context
Media education and equal opportunities.

What to do
Give each group a small sample of a particular type of material, for example, a couple of pages from a newspaper, or three or four advertising leaflets. Ask the children to scan the material and to underline the adjectives and descriptive phases used to describe men and women. Then, the relevant chunks of text can be cut out and stuck on to the chart.

When this has been done, help the children to identify any patterns of usage that emerge, and discuss the underlying attitudes that these patterns show.

Age range
Nine to eleven.

Group size
Small groups.

What you need
A selection of broadsheet and tabloid newspapers; writing materials.

Curriculum context
Media education and equal opportunities.

What to do
Explain that different newspapers have different conventions for the language they use about people and that these conventions might reflect stereotyped attitudes towards gender roles and towards the readers of these newspapers.

Give each group examples of both tabloid and broadsheet newspapers for a particular day, and ask them to scan the papers, noting the words and phrases used by each type of newspaper to describe men and women. For each gender and for each type of newspaper, ask the children to compare the number of

descriptions that make reference to:
- career and public position;
- relationship to a member of the opposite sex;
- physical appearance;
- age.

Discuss with the children what attitudes to men and women might be underlying these different types of language. If you find that the differences are more apparent in the tabloids than the broadsheets, discuss what this implies about the newspaper producers' attitudes towards their readership. If you have a school newspaper, a similar survey could be conducted.

Further activity
Write to the newspapers about your findings, asking them to explain why they favour a particular type of description.

34. Male or female?

Age range
Ten to eleven.

Group size
A small group.

What you need
Writing materials, passages from books or newspapers using the generic pronoun '*he*' to refer to the whole human race.

Curriculum context
Language awareness and equal opportunities.

What to do
Let the children read the passages and ask them whether they consider the use of the male pronoun to be justified. If they do not, ask them what the alternatives might be. Encourage them to experiment by rewriting or recording the passages with '*he or she*' substituted, or a form like '*s/he*' or a new pronoun of their own invention. Ask the rest of the class their opinions on the revised versions.

Further activity

The terminology used for different professions is a rich source of discussion. Do we really need different terms like actor and actress? Why does a queen rule a kingdom rather than a queendom? Why is it that a woman can man a petrol station but a man can't woman one?

35. Connotations

Age range
Nine to eleven.

Group size
The whole class.

What you need
Writing materials, a chart of negative and positive adjectives (see overleaf).

Curriculum context
A language awareness activity related to a discussion of the media.

What to do
Show the children the chart below and invite them to discuss how they might fill in the gaps and extend it.

Talk about the factors determining which word a person might choose. Discuss how similar choices made by people like journalists, broadcasters and editors could affect the way we view people and events.

Note: Activities 32–35 are based on ideas in *The Language Awareness Project* by Angela Goddard (1989, Framework Press).

36. Colour connotations

Age range
Ten to eleven.

Group size
A small group, working in pairs.

What you need
Writing materials.

Curriculum context
Media education and equal opportunities.

What to do
Give each pair of children a sheet of paper with the name of a colour written at the top (a different colour for each pair). Ask them to write down as many words and phrases as they can think of related to the colour. When they have done this, ask them to classify these words and phrases as either positive, negative or neutral. Discuss the origins and the possible effects of such connotations.

	Negative	Positive
I enjoy eating. I am	greedy	appreciative
I enjoy talking. I am	talkative	sociable
I like studying. I am		studious
My house is tiny. It is	poky	
John doesn't talk much. He is		reserved

CHAPTER 3
Investigating phrases and sentences

Defining a sentence is an age-old problem. The traditional definition of a sentence as a group of words containing a main verb and expressing a 'complete thought', is both inadequate and confusing. Many perfectly good sentences ('How about a walk in the woods?' for example) have no verbs. As for the 'complete thought' requirement, many people feel that words or word groups like **Danger** or **For Sale** also express complete thoughts. The complexities of sentence definition should probably be left to professional linguists. The opinion of the Cox Report is that this is 'entirely inappropriate' for Key Stages 1 and 2: according to David Crystal there are over 200 available definitions (**The Cambridge Encyclopaedia of Language, 1987, CUP**).

Leaving definitions aside, there are interesting things that children can do with sentences in order to investigate how they work. The traditional categories of statement, question and imperative (or command) are used as starting points. However, the activities in which these terms are used should show that these categories are not as clear-cut as they seem.

Sentences always occur within a social context and usually within longer stretches of speech or writing. Accordingly, the activities encourage children to explore sentence structure by introducing them to the ways different types of sentences are used in public notices, rules, advertising, newspapers, sayings and the speech of younger children. Awareness of structure is also developed through games to compose, expand and combine sentences. The following information on sentence structure is aimed at teachers.

BACKGROUND

Phrases and clauses

Jack and Jill went up the hill.

Within most sentences, there are smaller units, called *phrases*, which hang together and have a single function: the sentence above can be divided into three phrases:

Jack and Jill / went / up the hill.

The various types of phrase are named according to the class of the main word or words in the phrase. In the example above, *Jack and Jill* is a noun phrase, *went* a verb phrase, and *up the hill* a prepositional phrase. Typically, a phrase refers to a group of words, but when one word can do the same job as a group, it too is referred to as a phrase.

Usually, our own intuitions about the way words work will tell us where the phrase boundaries are in a sentence, but sometimes there are complications. In the seemingly similar sentence:

Jack and Jill messed up their room.

should the division be 'Jack and Jill / messed / up their room' or 'Jack and Jill / messed up / their room'? If we ask questions like 'What action did Jack and Jill perform?' and 'What did they do this to?' it will become clear that the second analysis is preferable: *mess up* is a multi-word verb.

In sentences like:

Jack fell down and Jill fell down.

we have two larger units, linked by *and*. Each can be analysed into phrases and each can stand as an independent sentence. These units are called *clauses*. Sentences consisting of only one clause are known as simple sentences. Clauses can be classified into seven main types:

1. Subject + verb
Jack slipped.
2. Subject + verb + object
Jill dropped the bucket.
3. Subject + verb + complement
Jack was careless.
(The complement completes or provides more information about the subject.)
4. Subject + verb + object + indirect object
Jack gave the bucket to Jill.
5. Subject + verb + object + complement
Jill called Jack selfish.
(The complement here gives more information about the object.)
6. Subject + verb + adverbial
Jack lay in the mud.
(The main function of the adverbial clause element is to provide more information about the verb; it does not have to contain an adverb.)
7. Subject + verb + object + adverbial
Jill put the bucket on the floor.

In many of these examples clause elements consist of single words, but this need not be the case. Each element can be represented by more than one word and, in complex sentences, a clause element can itself be a clause, as in the sentence: *The boy who went up the hill yesterday has returned.*

These formulae represent the abstract, underlying structures of clauses. Actual spoken or written sentences tend to be a lot less neat. The clause structure formulae give us a general idea of the range of available structures in English, but they are not to be seen as models of what everyday language actually looks or sounds like.

Co-ordination and subordination

Co-ordination and subordination are the two main ways clauses can be joined to form longer sentences. In co-ordination, the clauses are of equal importance, and the commonest way of joining them is by using conjunctions such as *and, or* and *but*.

> You can have kippers *or* you can have porridge.
>
> Jack chose kippers *and* Jill chose porridge.
>
> Jack chose kippers *but* they tasted like porridge.

In subordination, a main clause is accompanied by clauses of lesser importance. The choice of subordinating conjunction, which can consist of more than one word, shows the relationship between the main and dependent clauses.

> We went up the hill *because* we needed water.
>
> We went up the hill *assuming that* the well was there.

Whereas the positions of co-ordinated clauses are fixed in relation to each other, subordinate clauses can come before or after the main clause, or they can be set within the main clause.

> *Although it was raining*, Jack and Jill went up the hill.
>
> Jack and Jill, *who should have known better*, went up the hill.

Sentences built up from co-ordinated clauses are common in young children's writing. One of the most frequently-asked questions about early writing is how to encourage progress beyond the stage at which children use the conjunction *and* to link long chains of clauses. Some of the activities in this chapter should help with this.

Subordination is a more complex process and it is not surprising that it tends to emerge much later in both speech and writing. A crucial point to bear in mind is that early attempts to use subordination often result in errors as children get lost in the more complex sentence structure, or syntax:

> The survivors of the shipwreck who were all cold and frightened walked along the beach was covered in driftwood.

The root of the error here could be that by the time the child finishes the complex sentence ending in beach, the intended shape of the sentence has slipped from her attention. This can usually be remedied by encouraging the children to re-read their work in collaboration with response partners. It is vital that in spite of such errors, attempts to use such complex structures should be encouraged as a sign of growth. Focusing on the error rather than the attempt could cause children to avoid experimenting with less familiar structures.

Finally, a word of caution. Progress in grammatical competence might consist, in part, of learning to use a widening range of increasingly complex sentence structures, but this is not to say that language which consists of such complex structures is necessarily superior to grammatically simpler language. Writing which retains the directness of everyday speech is often more effective than that which is grammatically elaborate.

Teachers used to insist that children give all answers in 'full sentences', a demand that usually ignored the fact that the relevant information could be expressed far more naturally and economically with one or two words. We must be careful not to encourage verbosity or grammatical complexity for its own sake. This means giving children opportunities to appreciate and practise the uses of language which is pared down to an economical minimum. We should also help them to detect instances in which sophisticated language, be it overly complex or overly simple, is being used to obscure meaning.

ACTIVITIES

1. Investigating notices

Age range
Five to seven.

Group size
Small groups.

What you need
Writing materials.

Curriculum context
A reading and writing survey.

What to do
Send off each group with an older assistant to collect examples of words, phrases and sentences from notices around the school. When they return they can be helped to read and sort these items. Key questions might include:
• Which items are telling or advising you to do things?
• Which of them are asking you questions?
• Which of them are providing you with information?
• Who wrote them?
• What are they for?
• What notices do *you* think it would be useful to put up?

Further activity
Encourage the children to contribute to a class scrapbook of notices that they see in various contexts. These can be photographed or copied and sorted according to location and function. Again children should be asked for ideas for notices that they think could be useful. Stress that the wording of such notices should be brief, practical and easy to understand.

2. Frame sentences

Age range
Five to seven.

Group size
Small groups or the whole class.

What you need
Writing materials.

Curriculum context
A discussion and writing activity that can be related to a topic on feelings. It provides a simple framework to help young reluctant writers to commit themselves to paper.

What to do
Write up frames such as the following on large sheets of paper or on the board.

   I get annoyed when..............
   I laugh when........................
   I feel sad when....................
   I wish that..........................
   I am afraid that....................

Show the children how you would fill the frames to express your own feelings, then discuss how they might fill them themselves. Use the children's responses to suggest appropriate vocabulary. Depending on the stamina and experience of the children, the frame filling can be done as individual or shared writing, and the responses consist of single or multiple phrases. Completed sentences can be used as a vocabulary resource or added to the children's personal writing folders.

Further activity
Frames can be used with older children to develop descriptive writing and more sophisticated sentence structures, such as:

....….is as pointless as..........
Cleaning your car in a snow storm is as pointless as teaching a cat to knit.

3. Ringing the changes

Age range
Five to seven.

Group size
A small group or the whole class.

What you need
Sentences cut into chunks and mounted on cards, blank cards.

Curriculum context
A brisk oral game to start the day or to play between lessons.

What to do
Take any sentence that the children will recognise. It could be taken from a story that they have been reading or writing, or it could be connected with some recent event. Cut the sentence into chunks based on the clause structure units described on page 78 and mount them on the board or on an easel. For example:

Yesterday/we/went/to Kew Gardens/and/Jatinder/got lost.

Have the children sitting in a circle and make sure that they can all read the sentence. Shuffle the chunks and ask the children to restore them to their original order. Then take any one of the chunks and swap it for a blank card. Ask the children to read the sentence, substituting any grammatically appropriate word or set of words for the missing chunk. The new sentence does not have to be true or even believable, as long as it is a recognisable sentence. For example

> Yesterday our whole class and some parents went to Kew Gardens and Jatinder got lost.

> Yesterday our class went to Kew Gardens and Jatinder was eaten up by a gigantic Venus Fly Trap.

Keep the game brisk by swapping cards after every four or five substitutions. When substitutions don't work, try to suggest modifications to the rest of the sentence that might 'rescue' the substitution. For example, if a child suggests *tomorrow* as a substitution for *yesterday*, point out that this will imply other changes later on in the sentence, and invite the child to make such changes.

4. Expressions you love and hate

Age range
Five to eleven.

Group size
A small group or the whole class.

What you need
Writing materials.

Curriculum context
A writing activity based on oral language that might form part of a topic on 'Ourselves'. This is a nice immediate writing activity for reluctant writers or those stuck for ideas.

What to do
Have the children sitting in a circle. Tell them that most people have certain expressions that they find irritating and others that they find pleasant. You will probably be able to supply some examples from your own experience. Go around the circle asking children to contribute one example of either type or of both. Annoying expressions are often easier to think of. When this has been done the children can write lists of such expressions, either individually or as a shared writing activity. Some examples may be:

Expressions we love
Home time!
Happy birthday.
Would you like to come to my party?

Expressions we hate
Are you deaf?
If it's not a matter of life and death, put your hand down.
When I was your age...

Further activity
Such lists tend to display a certain poetic quality just as they stand, but they can also be used as a basis for further discussion. Among the points that could be examined are the following:
• How many expressions are instances of commands masquerading as statements or questions?
• How many owe their disagreeable quality to the sounds of the words being uttered?

As this is a language phenomenon that most people experience, it is a particularly promising area for a cross age survey.

5. Playing with word order

Age range
Five to seven.

Group size
Individuals.

What you need
A sentence maker for each child, blank cards on which to write the chosen sentence.

Curriculum context
A discussion activity based on any of the child's own writing.

What to do
Write out and cut up into individual words any sentence composed by the child. This might be a sentence written independently, one that has been dictated to the teacher or one that has been composed at the sentence maker from word cards.

Ask the child to reassemble the sentence in its original order, helping where necessary. Discuss with the child whether it is possible to use the same words in a different order and still say the same thing. For example, '*My uncle took me to the dentist on Thursday.*' can be rearranged as '*on Thursday my uncle took me to the dentist*' (punctuation conventions have to be suspended for a while), but not as '*Thursday my uncle took me to the dentist on*'.

Some rearrangements might alter the purpose of the sentence. For example '*Our class didn't get much done yesterday.*' can be rearranged as '*didn't Our class get much done yesterday*'. This provides opportunities to discuss how word order affects overall meaning and shades of meaning in sentences, as well as conventions like capitalisation and punctuation.

6. Sentence slots

Age range
Five to seven.

Group size
Individuals.

What you need
Sentence makers, a piece of card with the child's own sentence written on it, blank word cards.

Curriculum context
A discussion activity arising from any of the child's own writing.

What to do
Begin, as in the previous activity, by cutting a sentence into individual words and asking the child to reassemble it. Look at the child's sentence and identify for yourself the places where additional words or phrases might be slotted in. For example:

∗ My § sister ¶ is ∫ lazy Ω

∗ Adverb or adverbial phrase: *sometimes, in the morning*
   Clause: *I think, my mum says*
§ Adjective or adjectival phrase: *little, wonderfully kind*
¶ Phrase or clause expanding on *sister*: *Jacquie, who goes to Crown Woods School.*
∫ Adverb: *disgustingly, slightly*
Ω As for ∗

Choose one of these slots and write out a word or words that you judge the child will be able to use. Show the child where to put the word and then discuss the change that has been made. Ask the child if a different word could be put into this slot. You should also ask whether it is really necessary to put extra words into the sentence: perhaps it is informative enough as it is.

When the child is comfortable with this procedure, help him or her to identify other slots in the sentence where insertions are possible by writing out appropriate words and testing them in various positions. Ask the child for his or her own ideas as to what might usefully be put into such slots. Emphasise that such additions are optional: their use depends on what you want to tell the person who will be reading your writing.

7. Conjunctions

Age range
Six to nine.

Group size
The whole class.

What you need
No special requirements.

Curriculum context
A quick oral game that can be played between lessons.

What to do
Have the children sitting in a circle. Start the game by reciting a sentence related to a recent experience the class has had. The sentence should involve the use of a particular conjunction; for example, '*We went to the museum but we didn't learn anything.*' Pass the sentence 'stem' around the group, encouraging the children to complete it in as many different ways as possible, the odder the better.

At the first signs of boredom or drying up, change the conjunction or the starter clause or both, always remembering to supply the children with at least one demonstration of the new structure before expecting them to contribute themselves. With children who are reluctant or who have run out of ideas, you can always try switching to *and*, the conjunction most frequent in speech and early writing.

When the children get used to the game, you can extend it by modelling more complex sentences with more than one conjunction, for example:

We went to the museum but couldn't go in because it was overrun with green mice.

> In the early hours of the morning, when everybody was asleep, old Farmer Johnson's fat, frightened little dog barked softly, when he heard a strange whisper coming out of the

8. Sentence stretching

Age range
Five to eleven.

Group size
A small group or the whole class.

What you need
Writing materials.

Curriculum context
An oral game that can be used as the basis for shared or paired writing.

What to do
Have the children sitting in a circle. Start off by reciting a simple subject/verb sentence, preferably related to a topic the class are working on, and invite the children to make it more informative by adding given elements. For example:

The dog barked.
• Add a word to describe the dog.
The frightened dog barked.
• Add a word or describe how it barked.
The frightened dog barked softly.
• Can we swap *the* for a phrase telling us who the dog belonged to?
Old Farmer Johnson's frightened dog barked softly.
• Why?
Old Farmer Johnson's frightened dog barked softly because it heard a strange noise.

Obviously, successive prompts given by the teacher will depend on the results produced by the previous prompt. The activity provides a context for the use of linguistic terminology like *adjective, adverb, conjunction* and so on if the teacher thinks that this is appropriate.

Further activities
• Sentence stretching is rather like building a tower with bricks: beyond a certain point the sentence becomes unmanageable. This provides an opportunity to talk about over-writing, redundant description and about how to edit written work.
• If the teacher or children are recorded reading the sentence as it grows, the play-back session will provide opportunities for discussing the use of punctuation.
• The game can be reversed. If the teacher starts with an overloaded sentence the children can have a go at reducing it step by step to its simplest possible form. Try to base the sentence on some experience that the children have recently had.

9. Riddles

Age range
Six to nine.

Group size
A small group.

What you need
A set of cards like the ones illustrated overleaf, blank cards, examples of riddles from literature and oral tradition.

Curriculum context
This is a more sophisticated version of 'Adjective riddles' from the previous chapter (Activity 13, page 59). It is a reading and reasoning game that older children can prepare for younger ones, and it can be related to any theme being followed by the class.

What to do
Give the children plenty of time to read, swap, solve and invent riddles before beginning this activity.
Spread the cards out in front of the children with the

Investigating phrases and sentences

> **Side One**
> I am shapeless, but people see all shapes in me.
> I am soft, though made of ice.
> I am water, but hard as bone.
> Though mouthless, I have many voices.
>
> **Side Two**
> Cloud
> Snow
> Ice
> Wind

riddle sentences showing and the answers hidden. Ask them to guess what the sentences are referring to. They can then write their own riddles on a specific topic, aimed at a class of children who are following that topic. Remind them that the sentences have to be short and vivid and that they should aim to create a feeling of mystery or contradiction. References to traditional riddles should demonstrate this.

Further activity
Children can be shown traditional spelling riddles and helped to incorporate these sentence patterns into their card games.

10. Body idioms

Age range
Seven to eleven.

Group size
A small group or the whole class.

What you need
Writing and drawing materials.

Curriculum context
A topic on communication.

What to do
Write on the board a list of sentences such as the following:

> Fred was all ears.
> Glen deserves a big hand for his work.
> John's put his foot in his mouth again.

Ask the children for their interpretations of such sentences and find out if they know any others. The important point to stress is that the meaning of each sentence cannot be arrived at by picturing what the words are actually saying. Instead, they are attempts to provide a vivid word picture of a particular situation. Children can try collecting such idioms and illustrating each one with a drawing of a literal interpretation. You could encourage them to invent their own body idioms and explain them by role-playing situations in which they might be used.

They could also collect idioms that use other types of imagery ('*Let's pull out all the stops*', '*Shake hands and bury the hatchet*') eventually building up an illustrated dictionary of idioms which could include some from different languages and dialects.

86 Chapter 3

11. Intonation and emphasis

Age range
Six to eleven.

Group size
A small group or the whole class.

What you need
Shared writing materials.

Curriculum context
An oral awareness activity that could form part of a drama workshop.

What to do
Write out for the children any sentence relevant to a current topic, for example 'Tadpoles eventually turn into frogs.'

Show how the sentence can be pronounced in several different ways by reading it five times, emphasising each word in turn. After each reading, ask the children to try to say what part of the message is being stressed:

• *Tadpoles* eventually turn into frogs. *(Caterpillars don't.)*
• Tadpoles *eventually* turn into frogs. *(It doesn't happen all of a sudden.)*
• Tadpoles eventually *turn* into frogs. *(They don't hatch out as frogs.)*
• Tadpoles eventually turn *into* frogs. *(As above.)*
• Tadpoles eventually turn into *frogs*. *(They don't turn into wildebeest.)*

Encourage the children to try this process out with sentences of their own, and to make up dialogues in which each utterance might occur.

12. Intonation and purpose

Age range
Seven to eleven.

Group size
The whole class, then pairs.

What you need
Shared writing materials.

Curriculum context
An oral language awareness activity that could form part of a drama workshop.

What to do
Write on the board a statement, question and command related to a current area of interest. For example
• 'We are going on a school journey.'
• 'Are you taking your computer game?'
• 'Put me on the next train home.'

Refer back to the last activity and explain to the children that in many cases, a change in intonation can imply not just a change in the emphasis of the informative content of a sentence, but a change in its entire purpose. Demonstrate this by pronouncing the first statement in three different ways:
• as a teacher giving an answer to a person asking why the children are so excited;
• as a parent insisting that a reluctant child should go on the journey;
• as a child who thought that the school journey had been cancelled this year.

Encourage the children to practise pronouncing the question and the command in different ways, inventing dialogues to provide a context for each pattern. For example, the question might be uttered by the following people:
- a teacher who was hoping to escape the noise of computer games.
- a child wondering whether computer games are permitted.
- a parent insisting that a child continue to practise computer skills while away on the school journey.

The class can then be organised into pairs. Ask each pair to write out a sentence and to exchange sentences with another pair. The pairs then have to make up two or three dialogues using the sentence they have been given in different ways.

13. What you say and what you mean

Age range
Seven to eleven.

Group size
A small group.

What you need
Writing materials.

Curriculum context
An oral language awareness activity that could form part of a drama workshop.

What to do
Referring back to the last activity, discuss with the children the difference between what people say and what they mean. They will probably agree that this is usually signalled by intonation, or the tune of what is said. Point out that there are, however, many cases where what sounds like a question or statement is really something different: a command, an invitation or an exclamation of disgust or approval. Ask the children for examples from their own experience at school. They may offer such examples as:

'Is that your pencil on the floor?'
'I can hear somebody talking.'
'That's right, go ahead and spoil it for all of us.'

Ask the children to make a list of such sentences from school, home and other social contexts, together with 'translations' showing the actual intended meaning.

Further activity
Many jokes rely for their effects on a literal interpretation of such sentences, for example:

Waiter, what's this fly doing in my soup?
It looks like the breaststroke, sir.

The children might enjoy working from their lists to make up jokes and dialogues that subvert the intention of the original sentence:

What's that coat doing on the floor?
I've been watching it for the last hour and it hasn't done anything.

14. The ten commandments

Age range
Five to eleven.

Group size
Small groups.

What you need
Writing materials, tape recorders, blank cassettes.

Curriculum context
A survey and writing activity that could form part of a topic on attitudes towards the school.

What to do
Explain to the children that they are going to research attitudes towards school rules amongst different groups in the school community. They therefore have to make up a list of questions which should be comprehensible to everybody from the youngest child to the oldest parent or teacher. Help the children to formulate these questions, writing them out as a shared writing activity if you are working with younger or less confident children. The questions may include:
• How do you think children should behave on coming into assembly?
• What do you think of the school's policy towards clothing?
• Can you suggest any additions to or deletions from the current school rules?

When the questionnaires have been compiled, send the children out in groups to gather their data. They should use the tape recorders to record responses from those too young or busy to make written responses. They should question ancillary workers and parents as well as children and teachers. When they have collected their data, discuss it with them and help them to select relevant responses on which to base ten school rules. The children should then write these out in a form which is simple enough to be understood by everybody in the school.

Further activity
Instead of condensing the data to formulate a consensus, the children could try writing out ten rules based on the responses of each group of respondents. They could then discuss the different perceptions of school life which these rules reflect.

15. Permutation books

Age range
Seven to eleven.

Group size
A small group.

What you need
Writing materials, an A4 ring-binder; if possible, a copy of *Find a Story* by Maureen Vidler (1974) and *Making Faces* by Norman Messenger (1992, Dorling Kindersley).

Curriculum context
A book-making activity, particularly suitable for older children who are designing books for younger ones.

What to do

Show the children the books by Messenger and Vidler and encourage them to discuss the similarities between them. If you cannot obtain *Find a Story* prepare your own version according to the following procedure.

Prepare sentences which can be divided up in a similar manner to the ones below:

The children in our class / go to the library / to hear stories and choose books.

Centipedes and woodlice / live under stones and logs / because they prefer dark, damp places.

Apples, carrots and oysters / can be eaten raw or cooked / and are both nourishing and delicious.

Arrange the sentences as illustrated and let the children see how the book works. They can then make up their own sentences, cut them into chunks and see if they work in the same way. Anomalous sentences will arise when singular subjects are combined with verb groups or pronouns from sentences with plural subjects, and when plural subjects are combined with verb groups or pronouns from sentences with singular subjects. Such anomalies provide a context for discussing subject–verb and noun–pronoun agreement, and for subsequent redrafting of sentences. This activity allows for the exploration of a great variety of sentence structures.

16. Mnemonic sentences

Age range
Seven to eleven.

Group size
The whole class.

What you need
Writing materials.

Curriculum context
A writing game that can be integrated into any topic.

What to do

Explain to the children that mnemonic sentences are useful ways of memorising specific bits of information. Write some examples on the board and see if the children know any others. Some useful examples are:

Big **e**lephants **c**an't **a**lways **u**se **s**mall **e**xits.
(Spelling of *because*)
Read **o**ver **y**our **g**ood **b**ooks **i**n **v**erse.
(Order of colours in the spectrum)
Every **g**ood **b**oy **d**eserves **f**avour.
(Order of notes on the lines of the treble stave in music)

Challenge the children to write similar sentences in order to memorise information relevant to the topic in hand. Remind them that the sentence should be short and vivid and that every word must count. Some suggestions for content are:

- Spellings of notoriously difficult words like *beautiful, whether/weather, thorough* and so on.
- Names of the planets in order of distance from the sun.

Further activity

As a short, regular exercise in fluency, challenge confident writers to come up with as many different sentences or acrostic poems as possible in ten minutes, using a given word or phrase as the 'template' for initial letters.

17. Brainstorming statements and questions

Age range
Five to eleven.

Group size
The whole class.

What you need
Writing materials.

Curriculum context
A discussion and writing activity to introduce a new topic.

What to do
Once you have decided on a topic, ask the children to produce as many statements as they can expressing all that they know about that topic. Depending on the age and ability of the children, this can be done individually, in groups with one child as the scribe or as shared writing with the teacher as the scribe for the class.

Investigating phrases and sentences

Now discuss with the children how these statements might be categorised. Write related statements on the board and draw lines linking them. This phase of the activity should provide a map of the children's current state of knowledge about this topic.

When the children have had an opportunity to reflect on this, ask them to discuss what they don't know about this topic and would like to find out. They should then write as many questions as they can to express this. These questions can be used as a blueprint for the study of that topic, with the children suggesting how they might best be answered, and monitoring their own progress by recording how many questions have been answered and how satisfactory the answers feel.

Further activity
Reasonably fluent writers can practise the punctuation and sentence structure of questions through a variety of short activities that can be done at the beginning of the day or during the odd five or ten minutes between longer activities. Some suggestions are:

• Give each child a postcard, each depicting a different surrealist painting, newspaper photograph or other type of puzzle picture, perhaps related to the current topic. Ask the children to write down five questions inspired by the picture and then to swap papers with a friend so that partners can write imaginative answers to each other's questions.

• Give the children an answer: '*Only when it rains*', '*Roughly circular*', '*Because the world is a funny place*'. Ask them to write out ten questions to which this may be the answer.

Such games should be kept short and brisk and related as far as possible to the topic being followed.

18. Sentence seeds

Age range
Five to eleven.

Group size
A small group or the whole class.

What you need
Writing materials.

Curriculum context

A short oral game to develop vocabulary with younger children. It can also be played as a writing game with any age group to develop fluency and to practise particular letter strings.

What to do

Write three words on the board and discuss their meanings with the children. These may be words connected with the current topic, items of vocabulary that you want to introduce the children to, or simply words that you think the children might find interesting. In the case of a handwriting activity, they might be chosen because they contain letter strings that need to be practised. For example, you may choose *magic, whisper* and *liquid* as the three words.

If you are playing this as an oral game, sit the children in a circle and get them to say any sentence they can think of containing the three words. When every child has had a turn at this, go around the circle again until every child has made up at least two different sentences containing the words.

In the case of a written game, set a time limit of no more than fifteen minutes and ask the children to write as many sentences as they can containing the three words. To contextualise this activity, you can set conditions such as the following:
• The sentences should be suitable as story starters, grabbing the readers' attention.

I didn't believe in *magic* until my grandma gave me a bottle of green *liquid* one birthday, telling me in a *whisper* that I should keep it a secret.

• They should be suitable as story finishers, suggesting a fascinating train of events in their wake.

So whenever I hear the *magic liquid whisper* of the breeze across the lake, I think of him and laugh.

• They should be suitable as core sentences in the description of an exciting event.

As the *liquid* spilled from the broken bottle, he began to *whisper magic* spells.

19. Proverbs

Age range
Seven to eleven.

Group size
The whole class.

What you need
Writing materials, tape recorders, books of proverbs such as *The Oxford Dictionary of English Proverbs* (1970, OUP).

Investigating phrases and sentences

Curriculum context
An investigation into linguistic diversity.

What to do
Write a set of proverbs on the board and see if the children have heard them before. Ask the children to try to explain what they mean. The important think to emphasise is that the proverb has a meaning which extends beyond its surface simplicity. *'It's no use crying over spilt milk'* is a piece of advice relevant to any situation in which damage has been done, not just to kitchen or cattle shed accidents.

Ask the children to collect as many proverbs as they can from their parents and grandparents, where possible tape-recording their responses, explanations of the proverbs and contexts in which they were learned. This should give the children a vivid picture of the importance of these oral traditions, particularly in schools where there are families from cultures which still value proverbs highly.

When the children have become familiar with the form and function of proverbs, you can encourage them to try making up their own. Remind them that they should take the form of short sentences expressing some kind of general truth. It might be helpful to start by giving them traditional proverbs which they can then update. You may end up with such modern versions as:

Always click save before you click quit.
(Look before you leap.)
Give him enough watts and he'll deafen himself.
(Give him enough rope and he'll hang himself.)
You can't teach a hedgehog the Green Cross Code.
(A leopard can't change its spots.)

Further activity
The children can then try imitating the rhythmic patterns of more traditional proverbs. The see-saw pattern of many of them, in which the content of the first half of the sentence is balanced by that of the second half, is relatively easy for confident writers to grasp. Some examples of these include '*He who never stumbled never walked*', '*Better to feast on gruel than fast on cake*' and '*Cold bones make hot soup*'.

20. Proverbs (2)

Age range
Nine to eleven.

Group size
A small group.

What you need
No special requirements.

Curriculum context
An oral activity to deepen awareness of the potential levels of meaning in sentences. It is aimed at older children who have already done the previous activity.

What to do
Write the following sentence on the board:

A two wheeled bike can't run on one.

Ask the children what they think the sentence might mean. If they have forgotten their previous work on proverbs, they might reply that it refers to the difficulty of riding a one-wheeled bicycle. Now, explain that the sentence was spoken by a grandparent to a relative who was about to leave the house after having only one cup of tea. Ask them to provide an interpretation given this context.

Now ask the children for contexts and explanations for the following:
- You can't fit two feet into one shoe.
- Never go boating with a drowned sailor.

When this has been done, do the same for the following:
- A table has four legs.
- Paper burns more easily than stone.
- Fish live in water.

The children should be able to see that any general statement, uttered in a particular context, can be interpreted as implying some kind of advice or moral. They might enjoy making up their own perfectly mundane sentences and inventing 'profound' interpretations of them.

21. Sentence slots (2)

Age range
Seven to nine.

Group size
A small group.

What you need
Sentences from children's writing, cards of several different colours, scissors, adhesive.

Curriculum context
A discussion activity based on the children's own writing.

What to do
Take a simple sentence written by one of the group and decide which of the basic structures mentioned in the introduction it represents (see page 78). Cut the sentence into units based on this structure and mount each unit on to colour-coded card.

A possible sentence may be:

The three witches / were / wise but cruel.

which can be divided into subject/verb/complement and each unit mounted on red, blue and green card respectively.

Give the cards to the children and ask them to rearrange them in as many ways as possible, discussing the following points:
- Which rearrangements result in changes of meaning or purpose?
- Which rearrangements don't work as sensible sentences?
- Which cards can be left out of a particular sentence without the sentence becoming 'unworkable'?
- Which rearrangements are more likely to occur in written, spoken, formal and informal language?

For example, '*Wise but cruel were the witches*' and '*The witches were wise but cruel*' are both good sentences, but do they mean exactly the same thing? In what contexts are you more likely to find the different forms? What about '*Wise but cruel the witches were*'?

When the children have done this a few times, you can encourage them to write their own words and phrases for the coloured cards. These can then be checked to see if they work in context.

Although the colour coding should serve as an introduction to the idea that particular word groups in particular positions do particular jobs in the sentence, at this stage it is probably not a good idea to introduce terms like *subject, object* and *complement*. Many of the children's own workable additions to the cards will blur these barriers anyway. For example, a green card with the phrase *living in the forest* will produce an acceptable substitution for *wise but cruel*, but changes the sentence from subject/verb/complement to subject/verb/adverbial.

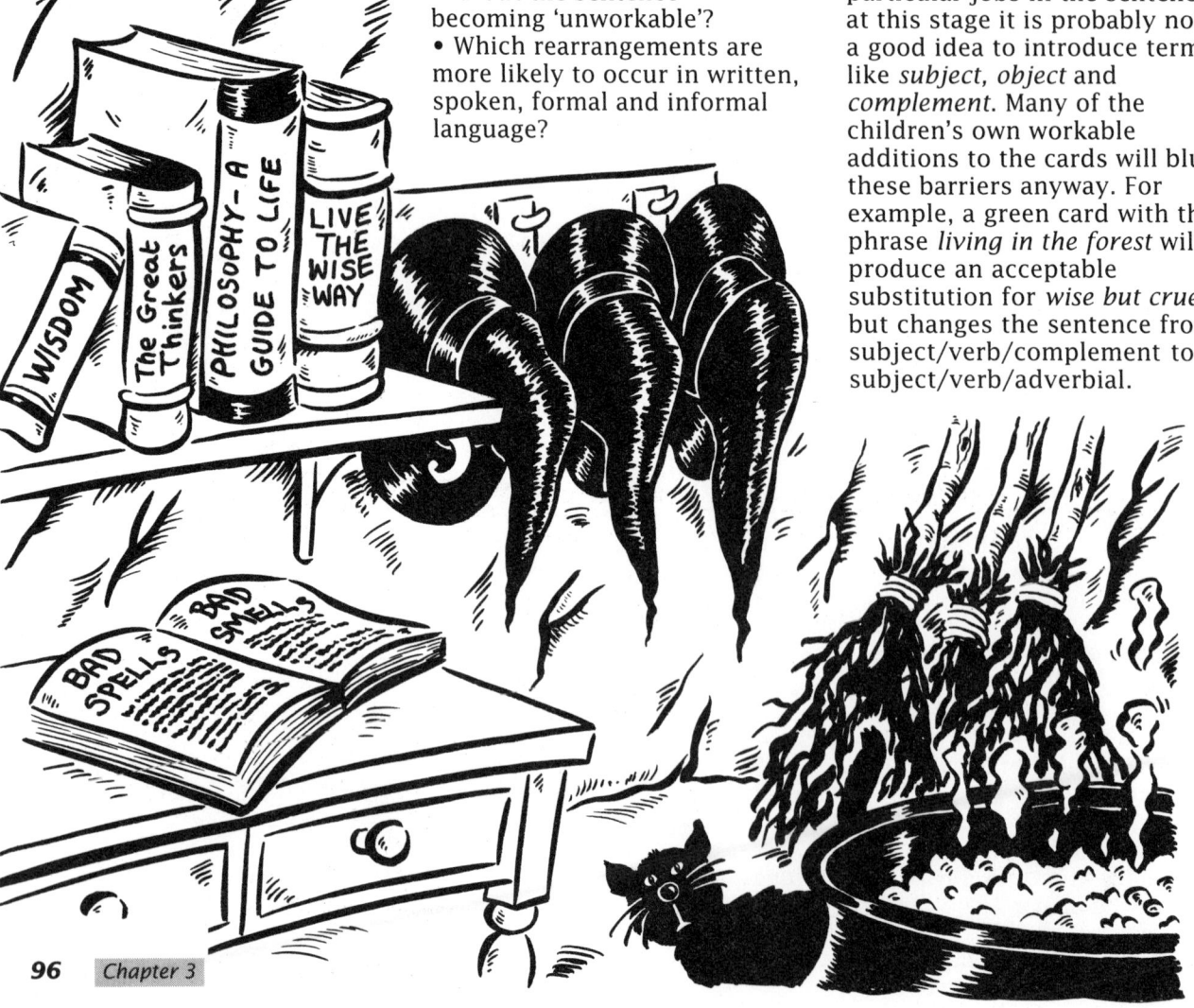

22. Sentence slots (3)

Age range
Nine to eleven.

Group size
A small group.

What you need
Sentences from children's writing, cards of various colours (some with expansion clauses already written on), scissors, adhesive.

Curriculum context
A discussion activity based on the children's own writing.

What to do
As with the previous activity, cut the sentence up according to its clause structure and mount it on to colour-coded cards.

The children can then proceed as for the previous activity. When they are familiar with this, give them the set of cards with phrases and clauses suitable to expand the sentence, such as:
• on the school journey;
• to practise survival skills;
• with materials we had collected ourselves;
• all on our own.

You could also introduce a smaller card with a carat symbol (^) and ask them to indicate where in the sentence these extra groups of words can be slotted. Ask them to suggest similar groups themselves and discuss which colour cards they should be written out on.

Further activity
Phrases like the ones above can all be added to the sentence without any conjunctions. For the next step in the activity, give the children a set of coloured cards with co-ordinators (*and, but, or*) and a differently coloured set bearing subordinators (*when, because, although, while, after*). You should then ask the children to find slots in the sentence for these conjunctions, and to supply appropriate word groups to follow them.

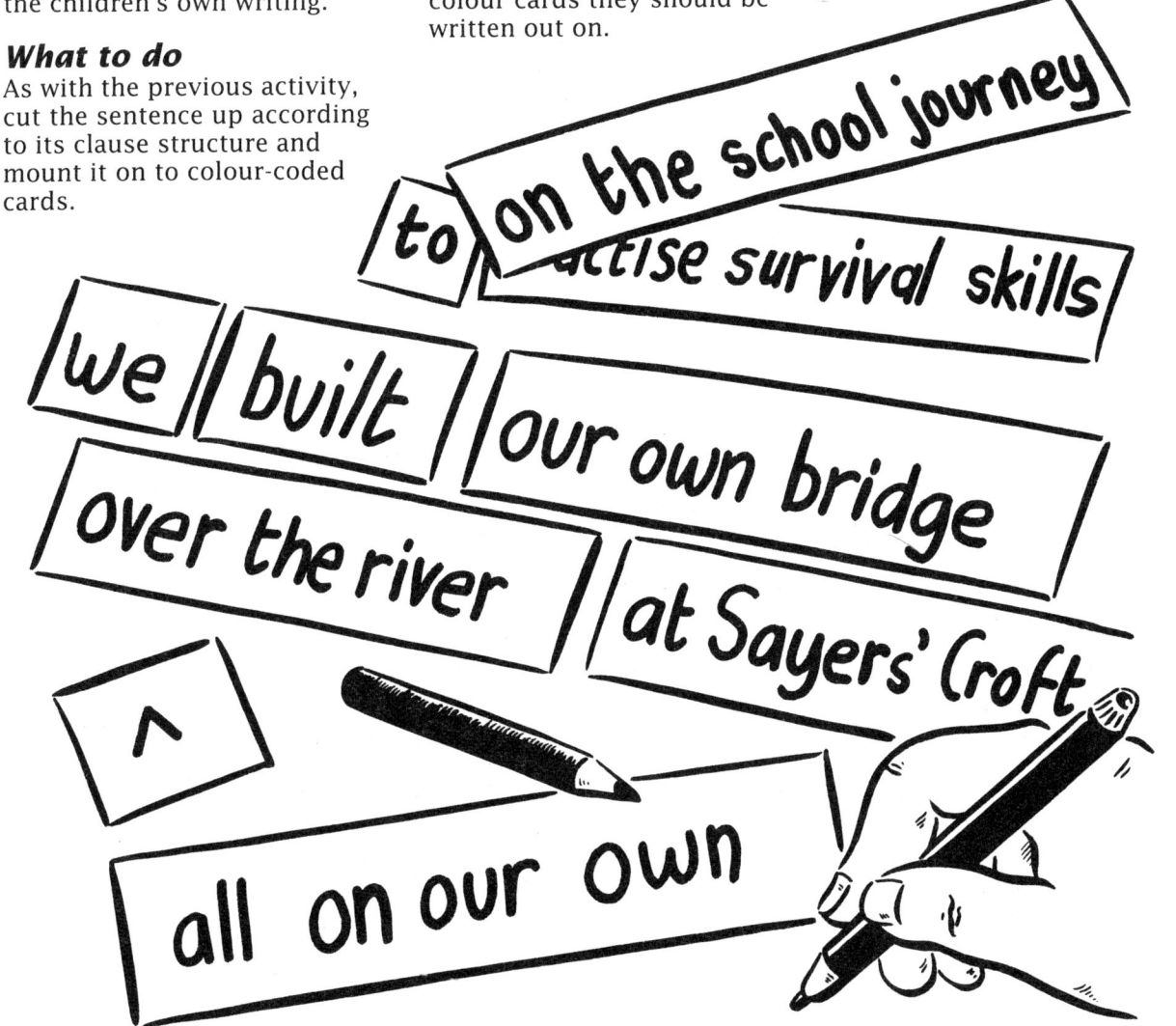

Investigating phrases and sentences

23. Grammatical consequences (Exquisite corpse)

Age range
Seven to eleven.

Group size
A small group or the whole class divided into subgroups of six.

What you need
Writing materials.

Curriculum context
A quick writing game that can be played at odd times and the results preserved for more extended activities at a later date.

What to do
Ask the children to divide their paper into six numbered columns. Do the same thing yourself on the board. In the first column, write a list of random adjectives and ask the children to do the same. When they have done this, ask them to fold the first column under and to pass their papers on. In the second column write a list of nouns, ask the children to do the same and to fold their papers before passing them on again. Continue according to the format opposite until all the columns have been used. This phase of the activity provides an opportunity to teach the children some of the terminology of parts of speech if they are not already familiar with it.

When all of the spaces have been filled, the children can open up the papers. Ask them to read the sentences which have been created, inserting appropriate articles (*the, a* or *an*) where they are needed.

Such sentences can often have an appealingly bizarre quality, an effect that has given this activity 'old chestnut' status in many classrooms. Its value for providing children with insights into grammar can only be brought out if the resulting sentences are discussed in detail. Some starting points are suggested below. They are aimed at older children who are confident readers and writers.

adjective	noun	adverb	verb	adjective	noun
green	pig	angrily	ate	noisy	plug hole
tiny	machine	carefully	ran	stagnant	soil
frightened	computer	quickly	read	dangerous	island
hungry	potato	cruelly	poked	happy	weather
soft	wheels	bravely	burned	sick	mice
moist	radio	lazily	defended	hopeless	cathedral

- What other words can be used to fill the slots taken up by the articles? Children might respond with words or phrases indicating number (*one, a million, no, some, many*), possession (*my, your, her, their, whose*) or terms like *this, that* and *which*. Does the use of any of these terms require other parts of the sentence to be changed? For example, '*Six moist radio(s) lazily defended which hopeless cathedral(?)*'.

- How many ways are there of changing the statements into questions?
- Are there any words in the verb column that 'sabotage' the sentence? Can the children think of any others that would do this? For instance, '*The green pig angrily ate the noisy plughole*' is a strange sentence, but somehow more acceptable than '*The green pig angrily went the noisy plughole*'. Why?
- If we were to increase or reduce the number of columns in the matrix, what types of words could we slot in or take out in order to keep our sentences acceptable?

Investigating phrases and sentences

24. Ambiguity and jokes

Age range
Seven to eleven.

Group size
The whole class.

What you need
Writing materials and joke books.

Curriculum context
A language awareness activity that could arise from the sharing of joke books.

What to do
Tell the class a few jokes of the kind which rely on ambiguous sentence structures for their effect. For example:

Last night I went sleepwalking near the swamp and got chased by a crocodile in my pyjamas. *What was a crocodile doing in your pyjamas?*

I once knew a man with a wooden leg called Charlie. *What was his other leg called?*

Ask the children for similar jokes, consulting comics and sources such as the Ahlbergs' *Ha Ha Bonk Book* (1982, Penguin) if necessary. Discuss the jokes with the children and encourage them to explain what they have in common and what their impact relies on. Show them how this can be represented by a diagram using either arrows or brackets:

(a man) with a wooden leg (called Charlie)
a man (with a wooden leg called Charlie)

Help them to diagram their own joke collections in this manner.

You can then go on to talk about more general instances of ambiguity and show how the double meanings can be represented diagrammatically. For example:

(Visiting) relatives (can be a nuisance.)
(Visiting relatives) (can be a nuisance.)

Ask the children to collect such examples on an *ad hoc* basis, and to look out for instances when such ambiguities might have a serious effect.

25. Jabberwocky

Age range
Seven to eleven.

Group size
A small group, preferably unfamiliar with Humpty Dumpty's definitions of the nonsense words in 'Jabberwocky'.

What you need
A copy of 'Jabberwocky' by Lewis Carroll, writing and drawing materials.

Curriculum context
Poetry and dictionary work.

What to do
Read the poem 'Jabberwocky' to the children. Re-read the first stanza and ask the children to visualise the scene which is being described. Encouraging them to draw what they see in their mind's eye might help here. Now ask them to attempt to define the nonsense words, and to explain their guesses as to the function of these words. For example, why are we so sure that *gyre* and *gimble* are verbs, in spite of the fact that we are unsure of their precise meaning? What variety of meaning can we give to a word which follows the word *Twas*? How do we know that *mimsy* is an adjective?

The children can then read Humpty Dumpty's definitions of these terms (*Alice Through the Looking Glass*, 1989, Dragon's World) and compare them with their own definitions. When they have done this, you can encourage them to rewrite this stanza, keeping to the same metre and sentence pattern, and substituting nonsense words of their own creation.

26. Definitions

Age range
Seven to eleven.

Group size
A small group.

What you need
Writing materials, dictionaries of the type which provide illustrative sentences to clarify definitions.

Curriculum context
Creative writing and dictionary work. This activity can grow out of the previous one, or can follow any of the word-making activities in Chapters 1 and 2.

What to do
Write a selection of nonsense words on the board. They can be made up for the occasion or taken from any of the activities mentioned above. Try to ensure that the structure of some of the words gives clues to the word class. Some possible nonsense words are *quobblist, prargly, moom, snuppy, wongulish*.

Explain to the children that these words are looking for a meaning. Suggest that they say the words to themselves and then try to imagine what they might mean. When they have decided on a possible meaning for each word, tell them to look at the way in which words are defined in their dictionaries. Using this pattern, they should write out their own definitions and provide an illustrative sentence for each one. When they have done this, ask them to swap sentences and to establish whether their partner is able to tell the meaning of the word from the sentence that has been written. If not, the sentence must be redrafted.

This activity provides another opportunity for teaching children terms like *noun*, *verb* and *adjective*. Knowledge of such terms is essential if their definitions are to look authentic.

Further activity
This activity provides an opportunity to teach the children about the citation form of words, that is, the form of the word that heads its dictionary definition.

27. Descriptive phrases, clauses and sentences

Age range
Seven to eleven.

Group size
The whole class.

What you need
Adjective thesaurus prepared in other activities (see Chapter 2, page 58), writing materials.

Curriculum context
A whole class writing game which could also be played with small groups of children as part of a Writer's Workshop programme of activities.

What to do
Refer the children to the thesaurus and explain that writing can be enlivened by descriptive phrases as well as by descriptive words. Read out some examples from favourite stories. Let the children select

adjectives from their thesaurus then incorporate these adjectives into sentence stems. The children should then try to finish off these sentences in as exaggerated way as they can. For example:

> I was so hungry that...
> ...I nearly swallowed myself.
> ...my stomach could be heard on the far side of the moon.
> ...I would gladly have eaten a dead rat in an old shoe.

Further activities
• Write a short story which is full of such exaggerated language. *A Treasury of American Folklore* (1944, Crown) is a good source of such tall stories.
• When might it *not* be appropriate to use such exaggerated language?
• Show the children a list of simile clichés like the ones below:

> as cool as a cucumber
> as bold as brass
> as sly as a fox
> as wise as an owl
> as bright as a button

Ask them to rewrite these similes as vividly as they can.

28. Grandiloquence and circumlocution

Age range
Nine to eleven.

Group size
A small group.

What you need
Writing materials, examples of inflated language.

Curriculum context
A topic on communication.

What to do
Write sentences of the following kind on the board, and ask the children for translations:

I would be honoured were you to grant me the pleasure of your esteemed company.

Due to circumstances beyond our control, there will be a withdrawal of the refreshment facilities on the 8.25 Wolverhampton service.

We regret that the children's library service has been suspended until further notice.

Encourage the children to try to pinpoint the main features of such messages. Depending on age and experience, they might spot the following patterns:
• long words are often used instead of short words;
• 'softening up' tactics, such as apology and flattery;
• the use of set phrases (*due to circumstances...*);
• the use of several words where one word would do (*refreshment facilities* instead of *buffet*);
• the use of the passive voice (*have been suspended* rather than *the council has suspended*);

Investigating phrases and sentences 105

- nominalisation: the use of nouns rather than verbs to carry the weight of the message (*there has been a withdrawal* rather than *we have withdrawn*).

Ask the children why they think people use this type of language. Explain that, as with euphemism (Chapter 2, page 67), the motivation may not be entirely dishonest. The desire to be polite or to show off may also play a part.

The children can be encouraged to collect examples of such language from literature and the media. They may also like to try making up their own grandiloquent translations of mundane sentences, for example:

> Due to internal turbulence, I must urgently request your kind permission to visit the sanitary facilities of this educational establishment.

29. Headlines

Age range
Six to eleven.

Group size
Small groups.

What you need
A collection of newspapers or cuttings, writing materials.

Curriculum context
Media education.

What to do
Encourage the children to look at headlines from as wide a variety of newspapers as possible. Discuss with the children the form of shorthand language used by headline writers and ask them how and why they think this language has developed. A collection of newspapers and cuttings covering several decades would be a valuable resource here.

By reading the headlines together with their accompanying stories, the children can try writing out full versions of the shorthand sentences used in the headlines. For example:

Minister Falls off Back of Lorry
The Minister of Defence, Mr Ares Swashbuckle, escaped injury yesterday when he fell off a troop transporter while touring army ranges in Dorset.

Discussion might focus on the following points:
- which words are selected for inclusion and which omitted;
- the time frame of the sentence: why is the present tense used for events which have already occurred?
- differences between the vocabulary and word and sentence lengths of various newspapers;
- the use of puns, alliteration and other types of word play in headlines.

After conducting this survey, give the children newspaper stories and ask them to make up headlines in the styles of various newspapers. They could then extend this work to producing a class or school newspaper.

30. Telegrammatic sentences

Age range
Seven to nine.

Group size
A small group.

What you need
Examples of telegrams, writing materials.

Curriculum context
A short language awareness investigation that could form part of a project on the media, communications or child development.

What to do
Ask the group if they have had any experience of telegrams. If they have not, explain their purpose and show the children some examples. Ask them to try to reconstruct the original message. When they are comfortable with this, ask them to imagine situations in which they might find it necessary to send a telegram. Pairs of children can act out such situations in order to identify the information that

Investigating phrases and sentences 107

needs to be sent. The challenge is to convey that information coherently in as few words as possible. The children can swap telegrams with each other to test whether or not they have been successful. As with the previous activity, discussion should focus on what parts of the sentence can be omitted without losing the meaning.

Further activity
At about the age of a year to eighteen months, children's speech goes through a phase known as 'telegraphic speech', in which one or two words are used to communicate messages. For instance, 'Dindin allgone' could mean 'I have finished my dinner.'

Children with young relatives who are going through this phase could be asked to collect examples of such utterances and to bring them in for discussion and translation. This type of research is further developed in the next activity.

31. Investigating babytalk

Age range
Seven to eleven.

Group size
A small group reporting to the whole class. The whole class can be involved in data collection.

What you need
Written or tape-recorded samples of young children's speech, collected by children and teachers.

Curriculum context
An investigation that could arise from a topic on human development or communication. This activity builds on Activity 29 in Chapter 2.

What to do
Let the group read or listen to the speech samples. Refer back to the ideas mentioned in the previous section on telegraphic speech. Find some samples that show other examples of the economic nature of young children's speech, and ask the group to identify what the speaker leaves out of sentences, what is left in, and why this should be the case.

Children's awareness of the complexity of features such as tenses and plural formations can be raised by examining differences between the ways young children use these structures and conventional usage. Some typical examples from young children's speech may include, '*I sitted down*', '*Daddy runned fast*' and '*I wented to Katy school*'.

32. Attention getters in advertising

Age range
Seven to eleven.

Group size
The whole class.

What you need
A collection of advertisements from as wide a range of sources as possible, which use certain sentences and catch-phrases to grab the reader's attention.

Curriculum context
Media education.

What to do
Show the children the sentences from the advertisements and encourage them to discuss where they may have come from. In many cases this will be quite obvious, although few

Investigating phrases and sentences

advertisements these days have the directness of *Beanz Meanz Heinz*. More interesting are those cases in which the sentence gives little or no clue about the product, service or appeal. For example, what might the following be advertising?
- Serious food for thought
- Just how strong is your instinct for self preservation?
- Just patch me up and send me back out there.
- From your friends in the business...
- It's amazing what you can get for nothing.

Now, show the children the complete advertisements and discuss with them the ways in which advertisers use striking sentences together with graphics to 'hook' the attention of the potential customer. Can the children identify which of the reader's emotions the advertiser is appealing to: anxiety, compassion, vanity, the desire for excitement or the desire to save money?

When the children have become accustomed to 'reading behind' such sentences they can try making up their own for a specified product.

110 Chapter 3

CHAPTER 4

Written texts

Traditional grammar is often described as 'sentence-bound': it examines the rules for combining words to make sentences, but it does not concern itself with structures longer than a sentence.

However, sentences always occur within a context, and usually within longer stretches of spoken or written discourse. The meaning of the word 'text' has, in recent years, become extended to cover all such longer stretches of spoken and written discourse.

The characteristic features of different types of texts are determined by a number of factors. These include the mode of the text (spoken, written or some kind of mixture, as in a lecture), the subject matter, the purpose of the message and the relationship between writer and reader or speaker and listener. These factors interact to form various registers, or text varieties. For example a legal letter, a newspaper article and a conversation over a garden wall could all be used to convey similar information, but there will be clear structural differences between them, reflecting the factors mentioned above.

In school and in their everyday lives, children are surrounded by a great variety of texts, demanding their attention and often seeking to affect their behaviour. In the written mode, these texts include books, newspapers, junk mail, the print on food wrappers and the packaging of other goods, card and sticker collections, instructions, advertisements, their own and others' personal writings, public information notices and graffiti.

Written texts 111

BACKGROUND

From an early age, children display a keen awareness of these texts. Their knowledge of different registers is evident in the ease with which children can simulate telephone conversations, the reading of angry letters and the language of television presenters.

Very often, this range of registers is not reflected in children's writing. Some researchers into classroom language have argued that the range of writing children do in the classroom is both too narrow and unrepresentative of the writing that is valued in the world beyond school. It has been suggested that in the primary school the emphasis is on narrative, description and personal comment, whereas the 'real world' requires competence in written genres which are factual, relatively impersonal and generally more businesslike. See *Learning about Writing* by Pam Czerniewska (1992, Blackwell) for a discussion of this issue. Each genre (for example, a business letter, a project proposal, a report) has a distinctive structure based on conscious choices about vocabulary, grammar, length, layout and so on. Children are unlikely to be able to use such structures unless these are explicitly taught.

The danger here is that attempting to increase the child's competence in writing for a variety of readers and purposes might actually lead to the writing curriculum being narrowed down to a course in the skills required to produce just those genres which are valued within society.

Writing has purposes beyond the immediately practical. The writing of poetry, fiction and journals in classrooms has a variety of goals which might appear remote but are nevertheless real, such as expressing feelings, exploring themes and ideas and developing a general interest and delight in language.

The argument that children should be taught about the structural characteristics of a variety of texts is a compelling one, as long as it does not undermine these longer-term goals. If children are to become competent in creating and comprehending these texts, they need to become aware of the devices which are used in English to sustain patterns of meaning from sentence to sentence. Look at the following examples:

You want a garden where slugs and snails are as rare as rhinos? You want a garden where the only creatures eating your lettuces belong to your family?
You want *Slug'em*, and for £2.99 a packet, you've got it.

This is how to make gruel. Fry an onion in a spoonful of suet. Season it with salt, sugar and cinnamon, then sprinkle in a handful of oatmeal. Add water, or milk and water, and simmer the mixture until it thickens. Keeping the mixture well stirred, thin to the desired texture with more milk and water, and serve hot.

Once there was a boy called Joe. He lived in a dull part of a dull town. He looked quite normal and his behaviour was unremarkable. He had friends who liked him, but did not consider him particularly special. His family were fond of him and regarded him as a good, ordinary, child.

Then one morning, while Joe was in the bathroom, he discovered that a fern had begun to grow from the palm of his left hand.

What is it that makes these sentence strings into connected discourse? Why do we read them as thematic texts rather than as random collections of separate sentences? We can point straight away to the use of a repetitive question structure in the first example and the list-like patterning and specialised vocabulary in the second. In the third, we recognise the traditional story opening, with its description of character and setting, and the attention-grabbing complication that tells us that the plot has begun.

More generally, in all of the extracts there are words that refer forward to what is coming in the sentences to follow, and words that refer backward to what has been introduced in earlier sentences.

This is how to make gruel. Fry an onion...

Once there was a boy called Joe. He lived...

These reference words are examples of the cohesive ties that link sentences together.

Written texts 113

Conjunctives or sentence connectors also contribute to the patterning of sentences. These make explicit the relationship between the information presented in earlier sentences and the information which is to follow. Some examples based on the continuation of the story starter are given below.

1. <u>Also</u>, a mossy green film had appeared beneath his finger nails.

Also is an *additive conjunctive*: the sentence it introduces reinforces or extends the theme of the preceding one. Other additive conjunctives are *moreover, furthermore, in other words, and, in addition*.

2. Joe was worried. <u>However</u>, he did not want to upset his parents.

However is an *adversative conjunctive*: it introduces information that creates some kind of contrast with what has been said. Other adversative conjunctives are *but, in spite of, yet, nevertheless, on the contrary*.

3. <u>Consequently</u>, he kept his fist closed and his hand beneath the table at breakfast that morning.

Consequently is a *causal conjunctive*: it indicates that what follows is a result of what has gone before. Other causative conjunctives are *so, because of this, hence, therefore, as a result*.

4. <u>After</u> an uncomfortable half hour, Joe returned to his bedroom where he made another alarming discovery.

After is a *temporal conjunctive*: it indicates the time relationship between the sentences. Other temporal conjunctives are *eventually, at last, suddenly, later, then, before, subsequently, earlier*.

Reference and conjunctive words contribute to the 'texture' of texts by doing specific structural jobs. However, this texture is also built up by the occurrence in adjacent sentences of interrelated words which identify the subject matter. For example, in the gruel recipe above the close proximity of verbs like *fry, season, sprinkle, simmer, thicken, stir* and *serve* set up and maintain expectations about the subject matter of the text in much the same way as, for example, a concentration of words like *sunshine, sand, sea, sangria* and so on in travel advertisements attempts to establish an appropriate mood in the reader.

As well as these devices there are 'larger shapes' in texts which give them their distinctive identities. Most of the stories that children will experience are likely to be chronological movements from an initial situation involving one or more characters, through a conflict, to some kind of resolution. Instructions are also chronologically organised, but consist of sequences of imperative sentences. Persuasive texts such as letters to a newspaper about an issue, typically describe a problem situation, contrasting it with a more desirable state of affairs, advance arguments for a course of action and conclude with a summary and recommendations. Information texts which describe processes often use the passive voice and omit references to human agency. Another grammatical feature contributing to the character of a text is the tense used by the author to maintain a consistent time reference or to disrupt this consistency.

It is important that children recognise and develop control over such features. Teachers can help them by including good quality non-fiction in the material that they read aloud to children. It is also important that these features should not be regarded as fixed and formulaic. Genre structures are open to change, mingling, play and subversion. For example, the gruel recipe above, which reads like an information text, could also be the opening of a historical novel. Similarly, information texts can take the form of stories or poems (as in the *Look and Wonder* series, 1993, Walker Books). Persuasive writing can also be expressed through poetic or dramatic forms.

This chapter presents activities which will increase children's awareness of the devices that link sentences together, and of the forms and functions of the various texts thus produced. Many of the activities require examples of the different types of text that children are likely to encounter in their everyday lives, so it is essential that teachers should build up a bank of such texts. This is a task that most children will be happy to help with.

ACTIVITIES

1. Card texts

Age range
Five to seven.

Group size
The whole class.

What you need
As varied a collection as you can find of cards with written messages; writing materials.

Curriculum context
A topic on written communication.

What to do
Show the children your card collection. This might include any of the following:

- greetings cards (Christmas, Diwali, birthday, Valentines and so on);
- get well and sympathy cards;
- congratulations cards;
- invitations;
- business cards;
- instruction cards;
- credit cards;
- recipe cards;
- card collections from tea and cereal packets;
- holiday postcards;
- membership cards.

Ask the children to sort them into categories, discussing the functions of each type of card that they identify. Choose a category that is likely to be very familiar to the children. Holiday postcards would provide an interestingly varied start. Point out to the children that although the messages on the postcards will probably all be very different, there are certain features that most of the messages will have in common. Try to identify those features by encouraging the children to make up a couple of typical postcard messages, perhaps suggesting enjoyable and not so enjoyable holidays.

Even such short messages will give you enough material to start a discussion about the distinctive features of different types of text. You could point out, using terminology appropriate for your children, features such as the tense and the typical vocabulary of the genre.

Let the children practise this genre by asking them to imagine that they are on holiday and are either enjoying themselves or dying to get back home again. They should then write down their messages, address their 'cards' and exchange them with a friend.

The basic pattern of this activity can be repeated with the other types of card to show the children the diversity of features in everyday texts.

Writing	Who wrote it?	Who reads it?	What's it for?
Bus ticket	Ticket machine	Passenger/ inspector	Proof you've paid a fare.
Reading book	Author	Children/ parents/ teachers	Helps us to read. Earns people money.
Note	Parent	Teacher/ headteacher	Explaining absence.

2. What's in your pocket?

Age range
Five to eleven.

Group size
The whole class.

What you need
Shared writing materials.

Curriculum context
A discussion activity to raise general awareness of text types or to introduce the topic-planning activity which follows.

What to do
Ask the children to empty their pockets and bags on to their tables. Do the same thing yourself. Sort the debris into objects that have writing of any kind on them and those that do not. Replace the latter. On the board, make a list of all the different types of writing that have been found. Ask the children to suggest categories for sorting the texts into different types or draw a table matrix like the one shown and let them take turns filling it in.

3. Comparing genres

Age range
Six to eleven.

Group size
Small groups.

What you need
Examples of texts which treat the same subject matter from different angles, for example, a programme for a football match and a report of the match; a TV guide summary of a programme and a child's journal entry describing the programme; a recipe and a description of the resulting dish on a menu; an advertisement for a toy and the set of instructions that come with it; shared writing materials.

Curriculum context
Media education.

What to do
Give each child a copy of the texts and help the children to read them. Discuss the differences between the texts in terms of layout, sentence length and vocabulary. Ask the children to think about who wrote each text, for what purpose it was written and how the different types of writing reflect the purpose.

When this has been done, use shared writing to create pairs of texts based on some topic of current interest. Here are some examples:
• a set of rules for how to behave in PE/an article for the school newspaper on the importance of PE;
• a 'manifesto' stating why the school has decided to develop a wildlife area in the grounds/ an appeal for parent volunteers to come and work on the garden;
• a set of instructions for feeding the class gerbil/a daily log of the gerbil's eating behaviour.

4. Story prediction

Age range
Five to eight.

Group size
Small groups or the whole class.

What you need
Any interesting story unknown to the class; a tape recorder, a blank cassette.

Curriculum context
Story-time.

What to do
Read the story to yourself before starting the activity and identify three or four points (no more), at which a development in the plot is signalled by a particular stylistic or grammatical device. For example:

> In spite of her promise not to use the key, as soon as her father had left...

> The wolf growled; he bared his teeth; he coiled up ready to spring...

> The sun was shining, the birds were singing and the children were happy. However...

Switch on the tape recorder and begin to tell the story in the normal way. When you get to the first point you have identified, stop reading and ask the children what they think will happen next. Make sure that they justify for their predictions based on what you have just read to them.

Read on, pausing at strategic points to let the children reflect on the accuracy of their predictions. It is useful to rewind the tape back to the point before you stopped, and to allow the children to listen again to the textual clues and their original predictions, so that they can judge whether the latter were based on the former.

Continue reading the story, repeating this process at each of the points you identified.

Further activity
Photocopy a short story from a photocopiable resource such as Scholastic's *Collections* series. Cut it into sections, breaking the text at points where grammatical or stylistic features signal a development in the narrative. Give the group the story one section at a time, allowing them to read, discuss and make predictions before the next section is distributed.

Alternatively, the sections can be shuffled and the children set the task of sequencing them.

5. Shared letter writing

Age range
Five to seven.

Group size
Small groups or the whole class.

What you need
Shared writing materials, a word processor, envelopes.

Curriculum context
A weekly shared-writing activity which should be linked to current concerns in any topic area.

What to do
Set aside a regular time each week in which you sit down with the group or class and write a letter about any area of current concern, preferably addressed to somebody outside the immediate school community. Some possibilities are:
• letters to the local council or newspapers in response to local issues;
• letters to members of the community, performers or writers, inviting them to visit the school;
• letters to authors, illustrators, television producers and creators of other educational resources that the children have enjoyed;
• letters to celebrities about whom the children are curious;
• thank-you letters to people or institutions that service the school.

Let the children choose who they wish to write to, and write the first draft of the letter to their dictation, pointing out salutations, page layout and sign-off conventions. As the children become accustomed to letter-writing, and depending on their confidence and experience as writers, you might choose to redraft the letter with them, taking into account the purpose of the letter and the degree of familiarity between sender and recipient.

Written texts 119

The agreed final form of the letter should be typed up on the word processor, and a photocopy made before it is sent out. The arrival of responses addressed to the class or group is usually an exciting event for the children. The stylistic range of these responses, from impersonal, mass-reply formulae to more friendly and informative letters, will in itself extend their experiences of a range of texts.

6. Writing instructions

Age range
Five to seven.

Group size
Small groups.

What you need
Shared writing materials.

Curriculum context
A writing activity that can be used to involve children in setting up the classroom at the beginning of the school year, or to inform the rest of the class about a new routine in any area of the curriculum.

What to do
With the children, identify sites in the classroom where there is a genuine need for a set of clear, written instructions. These might include instructions for the use of the computer or tape recorder, care of a classroom pet, organisation of the book corner or storage of maths or science equipment. Use a shared writing routine to get the children to compose the instructions in a form which can be easily understood and read back. This should provide opportunities to talk about the chronological ordering of instructions and the need for clarity in the use of referring words.

7. Sequencing instructions

Age range
Five to eight.

Group size
Small groups.

What you need
Any text that consists of a set of sequential instructions or directions.

Curriculum context
A reading and reasoning activity that can be based on the content of any topic involving this type of text.

What to do
Cut the instructions into separate strips, making sure that clues like numbers have

been removed. Explain to the children the nature of the task that the instructions refer to. If a list of ingredients is involved, let the children have this intact.

Give the children the shuffled instructions and ask them to put them into their proper order, paying attention to cohesive devices like the repetition of words, temporal words and the use of pronouns.

8. Fortunately, unfortunately

Age range
Five to nine.

Group size
Small groups or the whole class.

What you need
No specific requirements.

Curriculum context
A game that can be played at the end of the day or between lessons. It can also be used a prelude to story writing.

What to do
Ask the children to sit in a circle. Tell them a short story of your own invention in which alternate sentences after the opening one begin with *fortunately* and *unfortunately*, as in this example:

On my way to work this morning I was attacked by a Rottweiler. *Fortunately*, the owner was a friend of mine and told the dog to behave. *Unfortunately*, it took no notice of her. *Fortunately*, I was carrying my electronic dog frightener in my bag. *Unfortunately*, the batteries had run down and it didn't work...

Once the children are clear about how the two terms work, provide a starter sentence for another story and ask the children to contribute a sentence at a time.

9. Connectives

Age range
Seven to eleven.

Group size
Small groups or the whole class.

What you need
A list of connectives such as *however, moreover, furthermore, when*.

Curriculum context
A game to be played at the end of the day, between lessons or as a prelude to story writing.

What to do
Play the previous game in exactly the same way, then explain to the children that there are many words and phrases that act as signals between sentences, indicating how what is to come relates to what has just been said. This is best shown by demonstration.

When I was on my way to work this morning I was attacked by a Rottweiler. *However*, it was only a small Rottweiler, and I was able to scare it off by pulling a fierce face. *Furthermore*, I am so good at pulling fierce faces that I could have frightened a much larger animal. *Suddenly*...

Once the children are reasonably familiar with the way in which these terms work, the game can proceed as for the previous activity.

10. Scaffolding sentences (description)

Age range
As a written activity, six to eleven year olds who are confident writers; with younger children or less capable writers, it can be conducted orally as a starter for shared writing.

Group size
Small groups or the whole class.

What you need
Shared and/or individual writing materials, objects related to a current area of interest.

Curriculum context
A shared or individual writing exercise that can be related to any topic or subject area. It could also be carried out in conjunction with observational drawing.

What to do
Give the children the objects and allow them plenty of time to examine and discuss them. Explain that the purpose of the activity is to use a systematic written description in order to encourage careful observation. (It is also a way of practising sentence structure and conventions and like full stops and capital letters.) With younger children, and with older ones doing the activity for the first few times, it is best to conduct it as shared writing.

Help the children to structure their observations by asking a series of questions, for example 'How big is the shell in front of you?' If you are doing this as shared writing, allow the group to decide on the most interesting response before writing it down, demonstrating capitalisation and punctuation as you do so. If the children are working individually, allow them time to write a response after each question. (Again, discreet reminders about full stops and capitals might be given at this point.) You should also join in the activity, writing your own response.

You could also try asking questions that require imagination rather than observation, such as 'What might you use the shell for?' or 'What do you think it would be like to live in the shell?'

After each question and writing time, read out your own response and invite the children to do the same.

After redrafting and proofreading, the completed descriptions could be displayed together with observational drawings. This activity is a good example of the type of 'classroom genre' criticised by genre theorists. You are unlikely to encounter it outside the classroom, but it does offer an interesting context within which to explore writing conventions.

11. Scaffolding sentences (narrative)

Age range
As for previous activity.

Group size
Small groups or the whole class.

What you need
Shared or individual writing materials.

Curriculum context
Story writing; this is a useful activity for reasonably fluent writers who are stuck for ideas.

What to do
Ask the children to imagine themselves in a situation that you specify. This could be related to a current area of interest, such as a historical period, or to some familiar story. After setting the scene, the activity develops in a similar way to the previous activity. Give the writers a sequence of oral prompts, enabling them to build up the story sentence by sentence, as in this example:

Let's imagine that you're walking home one night on your own. Write a sentence that tells the reader where you were coming from and where you were going.

Written texts 123

How were you feeling that night? In the next sentence, tell the reader what you were thinking about as you were walking along.

Now, something strange is going to happen. Perhaps you suddenly hear a noise in the sky or see something peculiar. Describe what happened.

As with the previous activity, it is best to introduce this as a shared writing activity, and to join in the writing and sharing of responses yourself when you introduce it as an individual writing activity.

It would of course be tedious and highly restrictive to attempt to dictate an entire story in this manner. Once the story is well under way, relinquish control to the writer, allowing children who want to abandon the story for the time being to do so. Abandoned introductions which are considered promising can be collected into a book of story starters for others to complete.

12. Knowledge maps

Age range
Five to eleven.

Group size
Small groups.

What you need
Shared and individual writing materials, drawing materials.

Curriculum context
An activity to teach children to write paragraphs and structured descriptions. It can be integrated into any topic or subject area.

What to do
Give the group a natural object or artefact that has relevance to a current topic. Allow the children time to examine the object, discuss it and draw it. When they have done this, place one of the drawings at the centre of the shared writing chart or board and draw labelled arrows as shown in the illustration. Encourage the children to suggest words and phrases in response to the labels, and write these down as they emerge. Now tell the children that each of the arrows points to a cluster of related ideas. Help them to shape these ideas into sentences and write these down on the chart in separate paragraphs.

When the children have practised this kind of structured description through shared writing, they can try it out individually as a preliminary to independent writing.

Further activity
Another way of getting children to organise ideas into paragraph form is to use a thought-provoking picture alongside a set of questions. The example illustrated below might act as a stimulus for story-telling, or fit into a topic on animals.

13. Story grammar: characters

Age range
Seven to eleven.

Group size
Small groups.

What you need
Shared and individual writing materials; drawing materials; blank books for mounting work in progress.

Curriculum context
A writing and discussion activity in media education that creates a resource for oral and written story.

What to do
Ask the children to discuss their favourite, or least favourite, character from fiction, including comics and film. Ask them to visualise the character and to draw a picture. Then, using one of the structured description activities from above, help them to build up a 'word picture' of the character. If you do this through shared writing the first few times, you can demonstrate how casting the sentences in the present tense means that the language reflects the living presence of the character, as in this example:

Dakota is a very bold girl who lives on a strange slum estate. She loves telling stories and having adventures. She is very bad-tempered, especially when she is bored. I think she is tall and thin with stringy black hair and wild-looking eyes.

Based on *Dakota of the White Flats* (Philip Ridley, 1990, HarperCollins)

Give this creature a name.

What does it look like?
Where does it live?
What are its habits?
Write 3 or 4 sentences to answer each question.

The children can mount their completed work into a book of characters. They can also be mounted on cards and used as a resource for future activities.

When the children have had some experience of describing characters from fiction, they can make up their own characters, basing them perhaps on people they know and giving these familiar characters a few extra quirks and secrets. If they find this difficult, a few prompt cards with a name and an introductory idea might help, for instance, *'Mr Sticky, the man who lives down the drain'* or *'Uncle Christmas, Santa's nasty brother.'*

14. Story grammar: settings

Age range
Seven to eleven.

Group size
Small groups.

What you need
As for the previous activity.

Curriculum context
As for the previous activity.

What to do
Talk to the children about their favourite stories, comic series or soap operas. Ask them to focus on the environment in which the story takes place and to describe it in as much detail as they can. Choose one of these settings and, through shared writing, show the children how a description can be built up, as in this example:

> The white flats where Dakota lives are a block of flats that were beautiful when they were built but are now all run down and ugly. There are supermarket trolleys in the fountain and all the buildings are cracked. However, most of the people who live there are interesting and friendly.

As with the previous activity, the present tense is used to give a sense of immediacy.

The children can illustrate and collect such descriptions and start to develop their own ideas for story settings. These can be based on observations made in different subject areas, such as this one:

> Grungia is a roughly rectangular island. It is always very warm and

humid there. The soft soil is a brown colour and full of holes of all different sizes that look as if they are the homes of strange underground animals. All over the island there are circular forests that sometimes overlap with each other. The trees are bright blue and green and they shed mysterious black dust whenever there is a breeze.

(Based on a microscope observation of a piece of mouldy brown bread.)

With older children, you can use geographical entries in school encyclopaedias as a model for writing. As with the character sketches from the previous activity, completed descriptions can be mounted on card and used for story-telling activities.

15. Story grammar: conflict

Age range
Seven to eleven.

Group size
Small groups.

What you need
As for the previous activity.

Curriculum context
As for the previous activity.

What to do
Invite individual group members to retell their favourite stories or to give a summary of a recent story-line from a soap opera or comic-strip series. Show the children how the events of a story are often based on a simple problem that can be summed up in a sentence or two. Illustrate this with some examples from well-known stories, such as these:

• X who is rich falls in love with Y who is poor. Social pressures and/or accidents of fate keep them apart.
(*Cinderella, Donkeyskin*, numerous romantic novels and films)

• A great treasure is lost. Group X (the baddies) and group Y (the goodies) compete to recover it.
(*Treasure Island, Lord of the Rings*)

• X grants a favour to Y on condition that Y pays back on cruel or impossible terms later on.
(*Rumpelstiltskin, Doctor Faustus, The Merchant of Venice*)

Help the children to identify the conflict at the root of the stories that they have related. This will be quite difficult for the younger children, who tend to focus on the minutiae of stories without contemplating their general form. You can try to overcome this by saying 'That reminds me of a story I know...', telling a related version, then asking the children to identify what the stories have in common.

When the conflicts have been identified, the teacher can then refer the children to their earlier work on story grammar. Ask the children to work in groups of two or three, each child selecting a character card and the group as a whole taking one card for the setting and one for the conflict. The children can then use these components to create stories through drama work.

16. Minisagas

Age range
Seven to eleven (confident writers).

Group size
Small groups, working individually or in pairs.

What you need
Writing materials, story grammar cards (optional).

Curriculum context
A short writing game that can be used as the basis for further work in media education or drama.

What to do
Challenge the children to tell or write a story within very strict constraints. They have to outline setting, characters, plot and resolution in, say, one hundred words, no more and no less. This means that there has to be very tight control over sentence structure and over the 'units' of story that the children may have explored in story grammar activities.

Further activity
Give the children an outline of a story and fifteen minutes or so to prepare a performance (a straightforward telling or a narration with voices and sound effects) that will last exactly three minutes.

Minisagas prepared in this way can be used as the seeds of more extended drama or story-telling on later occasions.

17. Story paste-ups

Age range
Seven to nine.

Group size
Small groups exchanging work.

What you need
Shared writing materials; materials for making home-made books, several blank ready-made books; a word processing programme; art materials; completed stories that children have written with a particular audience in mind; examples of minimal-text picture books; scissors, Blu-Tack.

Curriculum context
Story writing. This could be linked to a topic on making books.

What to do
Type out each completed story into separate sentences. Shuffle the sentences and give them to a group which has not been involved in writing the original story. Ask the children to sequence the sentences and then to stick tentative arrangements of them on the pages of the blank books, together with first drafts of possible illustrations. (In publishing, this stage is referred to as the 'paste-up' of the final product.) Encourage the children to examine the published picture books, which should provide some examples of how text might be arranged in relation to illustrations. When this has been done, make sure that the group consult the writer(s) of the original story before they put their paste-up through the final stages of retyping, illustration and publication.

18. Working from starter, finisher and middle sentences

Age range
Five to eleven.

Group size
Small groups, working in pairs.

What you need
Writing materials. A set of sentences from a variety of texts, mounted on card and positioned according to their original positions in the text

(see illustration). The sentences should relate to a current topic. Those representing narrative text could be taken from the 'Sentence seeds' activity in Chapter 3 (see page 92).

Curriculum context
A writing and discussion game that can be linked to any topic.

What to do
Give a selection of cards to each pair of children. Explain that the sentences are the only surviving fragments of lost texts. Acting like archaeologists, the children's job is to reconstruct the original texts from the structure and content of the fragments. Draw their attention to cohesive features like pronouns and connectives, which will influence the content of the sentences that they are to write themselves.

When the texts have been completed, the children can compare different versions and go on to redraft and publish them if they wish.

Below are some examples of starter, finisher and middle sentences.

Note that using simpler examples and a shared-writing context, it is perfectly possible to play this game with the youngest infants.

Starter

- We had been waiting for it to happen all day, but when it did, we were horrified.
- Although not as fierce as its reputation suggests, the piranha is nevertheless a very frightening fish.
- 1. Ensure that all moving parts are free from dust.

Middle

- "I would rather eat my own eyeballs than do that," replied Chris.
- Queen Agnes was not, however, without her faults.
- 4. Add the honey to the mixture drop by drop.

Finisher

- And that is why, in Amboiland, the women always bite their husbands' thumbs when it is raining.
- This invention is still in use today, largely unchanged and still very popular.
- 7. Rinse the test tubes out thoroughly and replace all equipment and chemicals in their proper places.

Wild flowers   Series of 48 No 17

POPPY

Scientific name: *Papaver rhoeas*

Habitat: meadows, cornfields and hedgerows   Height 30cm–1m

The most striking of British wild flowers, due to its size and brilliance. The vivid scarlet heads bloom from June to September. The petals usually drop within a few hours, but leave behind an attractive seed case which is often used for home decoration. Previously endangered, the poppy is now enjoying a revival as farmers set more of their land aside.

Issued by Thirstea Ltd, Ceylon House, London.

19. Tea cards

Age range
Five to eleven.

Group size
Small groups or the whole class.

What you need
Sets of tea cards; blank cards (A4 or A5); shared writing materials, scissors, adhesive.

Curriculum context
An art and design activity involving reading and writing that can be used in any topic.

What to do
Let the children browse through the collections that you and they have brought in. Ask them to pay particular attention to the way in which the printed information is organised on the back of the card.

Set the children a theme related to their current topic and ask them to draft a series of tea cards following the same pattern as that on the published cards. When they have done this, check with the children that they have used appropriate tenses and vocabulary in the main section of the card, and have adhered to the note form of the other sections.

The children can then type their writing into a word processor and stick it on to the cards, which can then be illustrated and displayed. Alternatively, the writing can be pasted into a large album and the illustrations stuck in alongside.

20. Mini Encyclopaedias

Age range
Seven to eleven.

Group size
Individuals, pairs or small groups who have an interest in common.

What you need
Reference material and real objects relevant to the interests of the children; writing and book-making materials; topic-based children's encyclopaedias.

Curriculum context
A classroom research and publishing project that can arise from any topic or personal interest.

What to do
Explain to the children that the objective of this activity is to create a home-made encyclopaedia on a chosen theme. Show them an encyclopaedia on a particular theme and ask them to make notes on all the different types of writing that occur in the book. These will probably include the following:
- a title page;
- a publication information page;
- a contents page;
- an introduction;
- entries on different subjects within the topic, alphabetically organised;
- suggestions for further reading;
- a glossary;
- a bibliography;
- an index;
- a summary, blurb and quotes on the back covers.

Discuss with the children the different types of writing involved in each of these categories. Each one will require careful decisions to be made about vocabulary and sentence structure. If the children are working as a group, individuals can take responsibility for writing different parts of the book, although all the children should have some proof-reading or editorial role that requires them to make decisions about structuring a variety of text types.

The basic idea of the home-made reference text can be introduced at any level. Even nursery school children enjoy making thematic ABCs with title and contents pages, and 'About the author' sections.

21. Multigenre on book backs

Age range
Six to eleven.

Group size
Small groups or the whole class.

What you need
Children's paperback books; completed stories written by children; book-making materials.

Curriculum context
Media education and book-making.

What to do
Present the children with the paperbacks and ask them to list all the different types of writing that they can find without even opening the books. Ask them to decide who wrote each item and what its purpose is.

If you make photocopies of the front and back covers, the children can underline or highlight different text types in different colours, and write notes on each type directly on to the copy. The back covers of paperbacks are a particularly rich source of text types and children should be encouraged to pay particular attention to them.

Publisher's logo →

A YOUNG BUFFOON PAPERBACK

Wendy and Sarah are best friends until the day Wendy accidentally deep fries Sarah's pet goldfish. This mishap leads to a frantically funny chain of events eventually resulting in the total destruction of the whole universe.

A delightfully light-hearted romp through the sunny storms of childhood.

A R-I-Y Reader

The Fatal Goldfish was shortlisted for the Rockall and Chelm Children's Book of the Year Award in 1993.

Charlie Prince has written several other children's novels since retiring from the Gotham Piano Tuners' Advisory Service. He lives alone on his woodworm farm in the Blasket Islands where he is building a shed.

'...a splendid book for all non-readers...'
Books Reviewer

'...today's children truly deserve this book.'
Sudbury Chronicle

Illustrated by the author
UK £5.99
ISBN 0-131313-1313

Summary of the main events – present tense (not like in the book itself).

Series title

Background information

Quotations – always positive. Often less than a sentence long – might this distort the intended meaning?

"THE FATAL GOLDFISH" / Charlie Prince

General statement, invariably positive.

Mini biography of the author – past and present time frames.

Additional information

Written texts

When the children have become familiar with these different types of writing, they can practise creating their own blurbs, mini-biographies and quotes. Check them carefully to ensure that the distinctive features of each type have been used. Children can then incorporate them into the design of their own book covers.

Further activity
Food packaging can be an equally rich source of text types. Ask the children to bring in an empty cereal carton, which they should then cut up into segments each showing different types of text. These can then be analysed along the same lines.

22. Break the register

Age range
Seven to eleven.

Group size
Small groups or the whole class.

What you need
Examples of short, functional, written or taped texts that have clearly recognisable features: bus tickets, traffic signs, menus, price lists, certificates and so on.

Curriculum context
Media education.

What to do
Give the children plenty of time to examine the texts and to sort them according to function. Make sure that they have read all the printed information that may be presented. Discuss with the children how the function of a text is reflected in vocabulary, sentence structure and other features of layout. This can be made clearer by producing 'spoof' texts where there is a mismatch between function, grammar and layout, as in this example:

This is to certify that the passenger holding this ticket boarded the No. 46 bus at Letsby Avenue on 26 August at 9.37 am and paid the driver an amount of money not exceeding 65 pence.

134 Chapter 4

Ask the children to explain why these seem wrong. You can then give them other examples of traditionally-written functional texts and ask them to rewrite them, using vocabulary and grammar that subverts this function.

23. Autobiography and prediction

Age range
Seven to eleven.

Group size
Small groups.

What you need
Writing and drawing materials.

Curriculum context
A topic about ourselves or about time.

What to do
As part of a story-telling session, tell the children about your earliest memory and ask them to share their own with the group. The children can then write about this in their next writing session. This can form the first chapter of an autobiography. Subsequent chapters, relating major incidents in the life of the child, can also be orally rehearsed and written up.

When the child's account reaches the present, refer back to any work on character sketching that the children might have done, helping them to build up a picture of their own appearance, social situation, habits, likes and dislikes.

When this has been done, ask the children to cast their minds into the future and to make a set of predictions for the rest of their lives, based on

PEARLBRITE costs about a pound a tube at the chemist's. You squeeze some onto a toothbrush and rub it round inside your mouth, then spit it out without swallowing any.

It might help stop your breath from smelling and your teeth from going rotten.

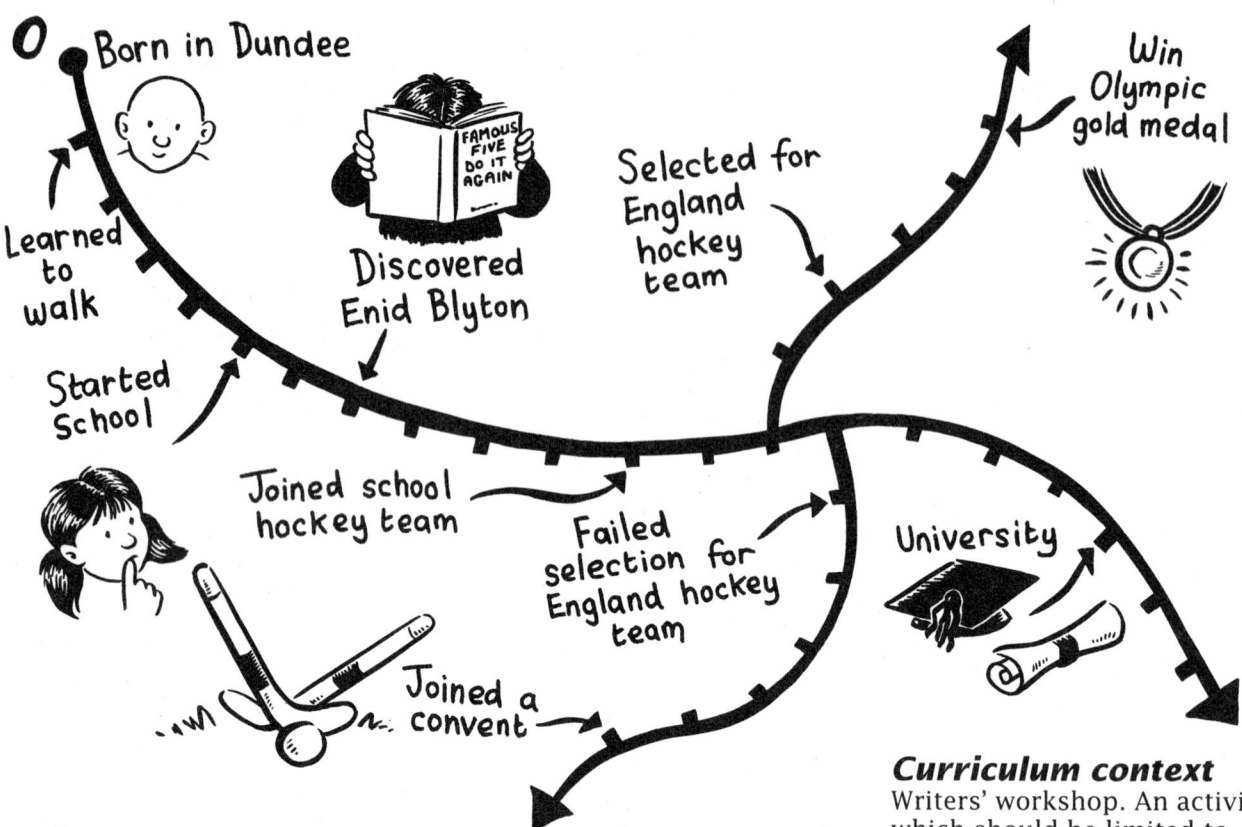

Timeline illustration: Born in Dundee → Learned to walk → Started School → Discovered Enid Blyton → Joined school hockey team → Failed selection for England hockey team → Selected for England hockey team → Win Olympic gold medal; branching paths to Joined a convent and University.

aspirations and anxieties. A time-line drawing, showing the past and different possibilities for the future, can be used to clarify ideas and plan the writing.

When the children come to write about their own futures, it will enable them to choose between and practise using some of the ways in which future time is indicated in English.

• When I am 28, I will emigrate to Australia...
• When I am 28, I am going to emigrate to Australia...
• When I am 28, I shall emigrate to Australia...
• At the age of 28, I emigrate to Australia...

Shades of meaning between the different choices can be discussed, together with other possible constructions (*I hope to, I would like to, I could*). The important thing is that once a particular structure has been adopted, the children should use it consistently throughout the relevant time frame.

24. Collaborative redrafting

Age range
Seven to eleven.

Group size
Small groups.

What you need
Short samples of writing, prepared by the teacher but based on children's work, photocopied for each child; writing materials.

Curriculum context
Writers' workshop. An activity which should be limited to those occasions when a specific group of children need to practise a specific skill.

What to do
Prepare a piece of writing that exemplifies need for improvement in a particular writing skill. This should not be an example of 'poor' writing, since it is never a good idea to present children with low-quality work. It should be enjoyable to read, but improvable in a specific way. For example, there might be instances of wordiness, ambiguity in pronouns, inconsistency in tenses or overuse of particular conjunctions.

Let the children read the piece alone, then encourage them to discuss its strengths and how it might be improved. Each child can then work at redrafting directly on to the photocopy. When this has been done, the children can compare their rewrites and negotiate an agreed final draft.

25. Cloze creation from children's stories

Age range
Six to eleven.

Group size
Small groups.

What you need
A story written by a child who is not a member of the working group; tape recorders and blank cassettes; writing materials.

Curriculum context
Writers' workshop or media education.

What to do
Take the completed story and record it in as natural a voice as you can manage, but leaving a pause of at least one second between each sentence. Then re-record the story on a double cassette deck, omitting sentences at regular or random intervals, and making sure that the last few sentences are omitted.

Present the group with the second cassette and let them listen to it right the way through. When they have discussed the story, they should try to reconstruct their own version of it, using the clues provided by the remaining text. They can do this by recording the story on their own cassette; alternatively you could provide them with a typed version of the altered story so that they can write individual or group-negotiated reconstructions. Finally, they can compare their own story with the original intact version and compare differences with the author.

26. Tracking cohesive links

Age range
Nine to eleven.

Group size
Small groups.

What you need
Photocopies of examples of narrative and expository texts; a non-cohesive text created by putting unrelated sentences together; coloured pencils.

Curriculum context
A reading activity that can be linked to recreational reading or to information text from any topic.

What to do
Give the children photocopies of any short text that they are likely to be able to read and

enjoy, preferably one related to a current topic or written by an author you have been enjoying recently. Allow the children time to read and discuss the text, then ask them to compare it with a text such as the following:

Andy Pandy's coming to play. However, the key doesn't fit the lock and there are only two moons orbiting Mars. The Battle of Hastings was in 1066. Suddenly, we all felt an invisible presence enter the room. It should have been a penalty. Have you bought your copy yet?

The children will probably be able to see that these sentences do not form a related sequence: the sentences which follow the first one do not refer back to the theme of this opening sentence, nor do they appear to share any theme at all.

Tell the children that they are about to investigate some of the ways in which the separate sentences of a text are made to hang together as a cohesive whole. Ask them to choose an important character or object from the text and to underline any word or group of words in the text that refer to their chosen entity.

When he was 50 years old, James retired from the Navy and became a tramp, wandering the countryside with all his possessions in the seaman's chest he pushed ahead of him in an old pram. One day a policeman looked at the battered chest and asked James what he had in it.
'A kidnapped ocean.' gurgled a watery voice from under the lid of the mysterious box.
James ignored the voice and told the policeman that it was just a box of tricks.
'A box of tricks?' the policeman said, 'That sounds suspicious to me.'

Female onchlids may be twice the size of males. The majestic female who leads the onchlid pack usually has a greenish tinge to her fur and is known as the Emerald Mama. The female skull differs from the male's in having pronounced, horn-like protruberances in the region of the temples. She also has more formidable canine teeth.

When this has been done you can help the children identify the different ways the writer carries the theme from sentence to sentence. An obvious way is through the use of pronouns:

the battered chest → it
the majestic female → she

Another way, which adds to the interest and variety of the text, is through substituting other words for the entity:

seaman's chest → battered chest → mysterious box → box of tricks

An awareness of the work done by such links might enable the children to use such devices more consciously in their own writing.

Here is my dog. It is big. It is not little.

Use any 12 of these words:—

a   the   for
and   go
he   then
I
in

a	the	for	out
and	then	go	saw
he	to	had	see
I	was	has	she
in	went	have	some
is	with	her	there
it	am	his	they
my	are	little	this
of	at	me	we
that	come	one	when

27. Texts with controlled vocabulary and syntax

Age range
Nine to eleven (confident writers).

Group size
Small groups.

What you need
Writing materials; examples of controlled-vocabulary and controlled-syntax texts from reading schemes.

Curriculum context
A creative writing and media education project suitable for confident readers and writers.

What to do
Let the children browse through the books and ask them what it is about the language of these books that makes them different from 'normal' books. You may need to help them to identify the limited vocabulary and simple sentence structures as key features. Ask the children their opinions on the use of such features. Do they think it makes a book easier to read? What about the effect on the story-line?

Now ask the children to write as interesting a story as they can, using only twelve words of their own choice, plus any twelve of the words in the following list:

When the children have completed their stories, they should take them to an infant class and test them out on some genuine novice readers.

Wendy Cope's poem 'Reading Scheme' (in *The Kingfisher Book of Comic Verse*, 1986, Kingfisher) should provide an amusing inspiration for this activity.

28. The Jolly Postman

Age range
Seven to eleven.

Group size
Individuals or small groups.

What you need
A copy of *The Jolly Postman* by Janet and Allen Ahlberg (1989, Heinemann); examples of all

Written texts 139

kinds of letters brought in by you and the children, including junk mail, official correspondence and cards of various kinds; writing and book-making materials.

Curriculum context

An extended project in media education which builds on Activity 5 'Shared letter writing'.

What to do

If the children are not already familiar with the book, give them plenty of time to read and discuss it. Tell them that the objective of this activity is to produce their own version, linked perhaps to a theme of current class or individual interest. For example, the Jolly Postman visits the inhabitants of the wildlife area or the Not So Jolly Postman visits those responsible for various sorts of pollution in the school neighbourhood.

Let the children sort through the letters that you and they have brought in, categorising them by purpose and intended audience. Help the children to make notes on the following features:
• the vocabulary used in the letters;
• layout features such as logos, mastheads and illustrations;
• the degree of formality or chattiness in the letters;
• the use of stylistic features such as rhetorical questions (*Did you realise that you could be the lucky winner...?*), direct commands (*Give now – don't wait for another forest to fall!*) and set formulae (*With reference to your recent letter, I wish to inform you that...*).

Let the children choose two or three different types of letter to write, incorporating the features you have identified as being typical of that type. Discuss first drafts with the children in order to assess, for example, whether or not a final demand for the payment of a bill actually reads like one.

When the letters have been redrafted, the children can work together on a verse or prose commentary, which can be bound with the letters and envelopes into a book modelled on the original.

140 Chapter 4

29. Campaign literature

Age range
Seven to eleven.

Group size
The whole class working in small groups.

What you need
Shared and individual writing materials; examples of persuasive writing in different formats, for example, letters to newspapers, petitions, posters and leaflets.

Curriculum context
A writers' workshop project related to any current area of concern.

What to do
Identify an issue that the children feel strongly about, for example, a problem related to the quality of the local environment, such as parking in the vicinity of the school or the need for more recreational facilities.

Discuss with the children who they might write to in order to improve the situation. Point out that there may be different purposes involved depending on who you are writing to, and that this will involve different types of writing. For example, in drawing the problem to the attention of other children, you are probably intending to enlist support and a poster, poem or song might be appropriate. When complaining to the council or government, a more formal type of letter might be preferable. Other possibilities might include an article for a local newspaper and a fable to be read out at assembly.

Ask the children to choose the format for their message and group them accordingly. Give each group examples of the type of text they intend to write and discuss its distinctive features before trying out the first draft. The persuasive power of first drafts from each group should be evaluated by the whole class before redrafting.

30. Who is responsible?

Age range
Nine to eleven.

Group size
Small groups.

What you need
Examples of texts in which passive constructions are used; writing materials.

Curriculum context
Media education.

What to do
Write imaginary headline sentences such as the following on the board:
- Martian found in the playground
- Martian found by school boy
- Schoolboy finds Martian

After writing each headline, ask the children to make a mental picture of the scene depicted by the sentence before writing the next one. Then ask the children to discuss the different types of information included in or omitted from the sentences, and how the word order affects the mental pictures of each sentence. How much terminology you introduce in this activity will depend on the experience of the children: key points are that the first two sentences are *passive*, in which the grammatical subject is *acted upon*, whereas the third sentence is *active*: the grammatical subject is also the *agent* or 'actor'. In the first sentence, the agent has been omitted.

When the children have discussed this, give them a set of news items such as the following:

- The school is going to raise funds by selling off the playground.
- The local council is going to close the library on weekends.
- A local business has donated equipment to the school.

Now ask the children to write three different headlines for each item:
- one omitting the agent;
- one emphasising the agent;
- one emphasising the person affected.

31. Jigsaw genres

Age range
Ten to eleven.

Group size
The whole class working in groups.

What you need
Photocopied examples of different types of texts, collected or prepared by the teacher, on a common theme: for example, a tabloid, broadsheet, TV news and eyewitness account of a UFO sighting.

Curriculum context
Media education, adaptable to the topic being followed.

What to do
Split the class into as many groups as there are types of text. Give each member of the group a copy of the text and let them read and discuss it. When they have done this, ask them to make brief notes on the following points:

- whether they think that the text was a written or a spoken one, and their reasons for their decision;
- which of the written texts sounds most like everyday speech;
- the length and complexity of the sentences (a simple word count would do for the former; an impressionistic account for the latter, unless the children have had a lot of experience in examining sentence structure);
- the vocabulary used by the writer – are all the words familiar to the group? Are there any words that they would not expect to occur in normal conversation?

- the intended audience;
- what was the writer's main intention in producing the text – for example, to give straightforward information, to entertain, to defend a point of view or attack somebody else's.

You should encourage the children to try to justify their responses to the last two categories by referring to the writer's choice of words.

When the children have made these notes, ask them to regroup so that each child in the new groups has been working on a different text. Ask each member of the group to read out the text that they have been working on. The children should then share and discuss the notes that they have made, paying attention to the similarities and differences between the texts.

Further activity

This activity should raise the children's awareness of how the writer's or speaker's intentions affect the structure of what they write or say. The children can be encouraged to respond to this in a number of ways:

- write a set of questions using the content of one text to challenge details of one or more of the others;
- write a letter to the author or presenter, doing the same thing;
- prepare a written or spoken text, taking a differing point of view from that taken by the text they studied.

The jigsaw idea can be extended to other types of text clusters: for example, groups might be asked to compare a menu, advertisement, recipe and health report on a particular dish.

32. Genre Consequences

Age range
Seven to eleven.

Group size
Small groups.

What you need
First sentences from a variety of texts; writing materials.

Curriculum context
A short writing game that can be adapted to any topic.

What to do
Give each child in the group a sheet of paper with the first sentence written at the top. Here are some examples:
- I am writing to complain about the noise from your party last night.
- Once upon a time, there was a farmer who kept three goats.
- When working with electricity, there are some precautions that you should take.
- Christmas was not always celebrated in the way that it is today.
- Day one: the seed looks a bit fatter, but nothing else has changed.

Ask the children to make sure that nobody else in the group can see the sentence that they have been given. Then ask them to write a sentence that connects with the one at the top of their paper, and fold the paper so that the first sentence is hidden, before passing the paper on. Each group member then writes a third sentence to connect with the second one, before folding the paper over to conceal all but their own sentence and passing the paper on again, as in the game of Consequences. Continue with this until six sentences have been written. the children can then open the papers, read out what has been produced and judge whether this is a coherent text. In some cases, the writing will be quite coherent, but in others there will be oddities resulting from a mismatch between what was written and what was invisible, as in the example illustrated.

You should encourage the children to examine the sequences and to identify what connecting features of the sentences have been used and which features have resulted in a 'breakdown' of cohesion.

33. Product promotion

Age range
Nine to eleven.

Group size
The whole class divided into three groups.

What you need
Shared and individual writing materials, examples of advertisements, instruction manuals and critical reports on various products.

Curriculum context
Media education.

What to do
Explain to the groups that they are going to practise writing different types of material related to an imaginary new product. Help the children to decide what this product will be; it should be related to some topic that the children are currently working on.

When this decision has been made, divide the class into three groups and explain that each is to have a different role:

> I am writing to complain about the noise from your party last night.
>
> I could not get to sleep until three o'clock.
>
> I was so worried about what the morning would bring.
>
> When the postman came I rushed to the doormat and opened the letter that he had left.
>
> There was nothing in it except a single piece of paper.
>
> The burglar closed the safe and tried the desk drawer.

- group one will write an advertisement for the product: this can be a straightforward newspaper-type advert with a 'hook sentence', slogan and information, storyboards for a television advertisement with text and graphics, a script for a radio commercial, or a poster where words are at a minimum;
- group two is to write an instruction manual for the product, aimed at the buyer;
- group three is to write a magazine article or consumer programme script giving a critical evaluation of the product.

Give each of the groups appropriate real examples of the texts that they are to write, pointing out the salient features of each. For example, advertising copy tends to be 'punchy'; wordplay is often used, as well as rhetorical questions of a manipulative nature (*Have you updated yours yet? How much do you really care about your family's health?*). Instruction manuals have to use simple precise language with great care taken over the use of pronouns, while some critical reports attempt to use unbiased language, often resorting to statistics (*On a blind tasting, over 80 per cent of our subjects preferred...*).

When the children have completed their texts, they should exchange them and try to assess how effectively they have reflected the typical language of these genres. Does the critical report sound fair to the advertisers? Does the advert sound persuasive to the manual writers? Can the report writers understand the instructions in the manual?

Written texts **147**

34. School language newssheet

Age range
Five to eleven.

Group size
The whole school.

What you need
Shared and individual writing materials; access to a word processor; art materials.

Curriculum context
A whole-school project in media education and language awareness.

What to do
Start by encouraging your own class to produce a regular bulletin which presents the results of any of the language investigations suggested in this book. This can take a very simple form: the children can write headlines and draw illustrations for the reports of their activities, and a selection can be complied into a paste-up sheet as large as the school photocopier can take. The compilation might include examples of jokes based on language play, items illustrating language and dialect diversity within the school and opinion surveys on controversial language topics.

The first edition should contain an appeal for comments on this content, and for similar examples of language usage, to be sent to a designated production group from your class. These can then be incorporated into the next edition.

As the project develops, it should provide a forum for discussion of issues in language, an 'exhibition space' for children's own observations and discoveries about language and a play area for recreational aspects of language like word play, puzzles and jokes.

CHAPTER 5

Oral discourse

It has often been pointed out that writing enjoys a higher status than speech, in spite of the fact that speech precedes writing in both the language history of the human race and the language development of the individual. The superior status of writing is based largely on the contrast between the fixedness of writing and the fluidity of speech. Because writing provides a relatively permanent record of the ideas it represents, it has always had powerful institutional and ritual functions which have been traditionally confined to social elites.

When grammarians began to study the regularities of language and to prescribe rules of usage, they naturally based their prescriptions on the patterns of written language, since this is the form that can most easily be analysed. Written texts are typically the end products of painstaking processes of preparation, redrafting, correction, reflection, consultation and editing. Everyday conversation, the commonest type of spoken text, is formed in very different circumstances. The participants who create its patterns do so spontaneously, reacting to each other's contributions, which might include interruptions, digressions, hesitations, questions and misunderstandings. They also have to show through various words and gestures that they hear and understand the contributions of others.

BACKGROUND

Some of the distinctive features of this spontaneous structuring are outlined below:
- fillers *(err... erm... well)* are used to mark the pauses where the speaker is shaping the next words;
- hesitation, repetition, false starts and corrections are common, reflecting the necessarily more rapid pace of oral composition;
- expressions are used which monitor the listener's understanding *('You know what I mean?')* and provide the speaker with feedback *('I see', 'Good grief!')*;
- informal words and expressions are used, some of which may be peculiar to the speaker *('I forgot to pack the tiddly-pom')*;
- reference words occur which cannot be interpreted outside the context shared by the speakers *('Look at that thing over there')*. The shared physical context of conversation also allows a larger amount of ellipsis or omission than written communication *('Coming?' 'Two minutes')*;
- there are more interactive forms like questions, imperatives and exclamations than in writing.
- sentences tend to be shorter and simpler than in writing, frequently interrupted by hesitations and parentheses. There is less subordination and greater use of connectives like *and*, *but* and *so*.

In addition to these features, speech also differs from writing in being far more open to variation. The way a person talks varies according to age, gender, social class, race and individual idiosyncracy in far more vivid and immediate ways than similar variations in writing. This openness is also apparent in the fact that linguistic innovation tends to occur more frequently in speech than in writing. New slang words and catch-phrases come and go with great rapidity, and little is ever preserved in writing. The conservatism of the written mode is most apparent in the English spelling system which has not bothered to reflect long-term pronunciation changes, instead representing speech as it sounded several hundred years ago.

These features have given rise to the belief that speech is in some way less grammatical than writing. This is an over-simplification. The features mentioned above, which might give a surface impression of formlessness when written down out of context, are in fact functional responses to the social interactions at work in any conversation. A conversation in which everybody spoke as if from a book with no pauses, digressions, parentheses or corrections would sound either staged or robotic.

There are, of course, types of speech which are closer to the written mode and share some of its more fixed pattens. A prepared speech or lecture is the most obvious example. There are also oral traditions such as proverbs and memorised stories which have the stability of written language. Conversely, there are forms of writing which have the transience of ordinary conversation. These tend to be forms like lists, notes and first drafts where we talk to ourselves through writing.

Speech and writing are not, therefore, polar opposites. Depending on the context, features typical of either mode can be found in the other. Two children having a row might be said to be using a purely conversational mode, while a solitary child writing an entry for a class encyclopaedia might be said to be using a purely written mode. However, even at these 'extreme' ends of the spectrum of spoken/written forms, there may be some mingling: insults exchanged in a row may be lifted from fiction or ritualistic tradition; while the encyclopaedia entry may be written in a 'chatty' style to make it more accessible to readers. These speech/writing interactions are reciprocal. When a child is first learning to read and write, the patterns of that child's spoken language provide the most accessible route into the new medium. When the child is familiar with written language, the rich vocabulary and diverse structures of this language will in turn extend the child's spoken repertoire.

The activities in this chapter encourage children to explore spoken texts such as conversations, interviews, advertisements, monologues and story-tellings. By examining the structures of these everyday events, children should become more aware of the distinctive grammatical features of speech and of the mutually supportive relationship between talking and writing.

ACTIVITIES

1. Talkhoard

Age range
Five to eleven.

Group size
The whole class.

What you need
Tape recorder; writing and drawing materials.

Curriculum context
A resource building activity that can feed activities in all areas of the curriculum.

What to do
Explain to the children that you want to make a collection of all the different kinds of speech that occur in the world around them. Help the children to make a list of these different kinds of speech, and ask how they can be collected. The obvious answer is through tape-recording, though simpler options include the following:
- books containing the typical remarks that people make;
- comic-strip records of conversation;
- single cartoons, featuring jokes and other short exchanges.

Ask the children to start collecting samples of interesting conversations, jokes and sayings and to record them in such a way that they can be shared by other members of the class. Once a week or so, devote some time to a whole class sharing session in which you listen to and talk about additions to the collection.

Such a collection will form a valuable resource for many of the activities in the rest of this chapter.

2. What we do with speech

Age range
Five to seven.

Group size
The whole class.

What you need
Shared writing and drawing materials.

Curriculum context
A shared writing activity that could introduce the school year.

What to do
Tell the children the story of your day so far, emphasising all the different ways in which you have used speech. You might include:
- greeting friends;
- asking for a bus fare, newspaper and so on;
- talking to parents about absentees;
- welcoming the children;
- taking the register;
- introducing the day's work;
- asking for information from children, parents and colleagues;
- telling a story;
- responding to questions and requests;
- talking to yourself to clarify thoughts.

Ask the children to share with the class all the kinds of talking that they have engaged in during the day. Use the board to record and categorise responses. The following categories might be useful.
- greetings;
- asking for things;
- giving people information;
- telling stories and jokes;
- playground games;
- responding to what people have told you.

The children can then make a display, drawing a picture to illustrate each of these usages, and adding a speech balloon with an example of the kind of talk involved.

3. Oral retellings

Age range
Five to eleven.

Group size
The whole class or a small group.

What you need
Stories, tape recorder, video camera (if possible).

Curriculum context
An activity that can be done as a follow-up to daily story-time.

What to do
On a regular basis, encourage the children to offer their own oral retellings of stories that you have read to them. These retellings can either stick to the original story-line, or consist of free improvisations on the original theme. When the children are confident about doing this, you can encourage them to research some of the differences between oral and written tellings.

In order to do this, tape-record yourself or somebody else doing a straightforward reading of a story. Then record a child retelling the same

story, keeping to the original story-line for the purposes of this activity. Play back the two tapes and ask the children to note differences along the following lines:
• features of the oral account which are not present in the written story. For example, non-standard words and sentence patterns, hesitations, corrections, filler words like *'well'* and *'so'*, direct address to the audience (*'you know how you feel when...'*) and repetitions;
• features of the written account which are not present in the oral retelling: more detail, a wider vocabulary, more complex sentence structures and more predictable pauses signalled by punctuation marks;
• features of the oral retelling which may have been imported from the written version: direct quotes, formulae like *'once upon a time'*, literary devices like adjective chains (*'She lived in a low, smelly, dark, shabby shack...'*) alliteration, simile and metaphor;
• ways in which the teller paraphrases the story, preserving the gist of the episodes but using different words and phrases.

If you have a video camera available, it may be interesting to examine how the teller uses non-verbal communication (gesture, body language, eye contact) to convey meaning. The objective here is to raise children's awareness of the relationships between speech and writing. They should appreciate that both have distinctive features and that speech is not an inferior reflection of writing.

4. Puppet tapes

Age range
Five to eleven.

Group size
Pairs.

What you need
Puppets whose appearance is open enough to represent a variety of characters, tape recorder, video camera (if possible).

Curriculum context.
A play activity that can be used as the basis for a whole class discussion.

What to do
Let the children play freely with the puppets before attempting to involve them in this more structured activity. Then, present them with the following minidramas:
• A teacher is telling a child off for damaging a book; the child is denying responsibility.
• Two adults are talking about a row in the street last night.

- Two children are trying to decide what to watch on television.
- A parent is explaining a child's illness to a doctor.

Let the children choose roles, show them how to operate the tape recorder or video camera, then let them get on with it. When a number of children have completed their dialogues, interpretations of the same situation can be compared, then interpretations of different situations. Ask the children to try to identify how speech changes according to the context. At this stage, such a discussion will be very impressionistic and strongly tied up with the particular dramas that the children have created, but these early opportunities to reflect on talk will provide the groundwork for more analytical activities later on.

5. School talk

Age range
Five to eleven.

Group size
The whole class, working in groups or pairs.

What you need
Tape recorder.

Curriculum context
A topic on communication.

What to do
Ask the children to think of as many different situations as they can in which people have conversations at school. As responses are made, write them up on the board. They might include:
- talking to a friend about what you saw on television last night;
- discussing the work you've been given to do;
- arguing with the teacher or with other children;
- parents talking in the playground or at the school gate;
- teachers' staffroom talk;
- talking with dinner helpers and other ancillary staff;
- telephone conversations;
- talk between teacher and children before and after a story;
- assembly talk.

When a sizeable list has been made, tell the children that they are going to compile and research a collection of such conversations. Allow the children to choose which types of conversation they would like to look into, and draw up a rota for use of the tape recorder. Each pair or group should be asked to set up the tape recorder where they are likely to be able to collect five- to ten-minute samples of a particular type of talk. (Note that the co-operation of the participants must be sought beforehand. If this is done a few days in advance of the sampling, and the precise time of the sampling left unspecific, there is more chance of you being able to collect spontaneous data. These issues should be discussed with the children.) If it is impractical to use a tape recorder in some situations (for example, at the school gate) you can use fluent writers with good memories to collect the data with a notepad and pencil. If you are conducting this activity with younger children, older ones can help out with the data collection.

When the children have collected the data on tape, extracts can be transcribed and displayed. The children can discuss the following points:
- who is 'in charge' of particular conversations? Is there a definite leader or questioner, or are the participants seemingly equal?
- the variety of languages, accents and dialects represented in the samples, and the contexts in which these varieties are used and not used;
- what differences in vocabulary are evident in the conversations? For example, educational jargon, playground slang, the terminology of subject areas;
- differences related to gender and to age;
- how people adapt their language according to whom they are talking to;
- aspects of talk which are difficult to interpret outside the context of the conversation. For example, remarks like *'Cut that out!'* and *'Put that over there and leave this one over here.'*

Children's reflections on these aspects of language can be displayed alongside the extracts on which they are based. This collection of samples and reflections might form the basis for a more extended, whole school project, such as a video film on the varieties of language to be found in the school and its surrounding community.

6. Angry and polite dialogue

Age range
Six to eleven.

Group size
The whole class, working in pairs.

What you need
Tape recorders; video tape extracts depicting angry speech for follow-up work

Curriculum context
A drama activity that could be related to a topic on communication.

What to do
Ask the children to improvise two related conversations: the first in a situation where it would be natural for the participants to be polite to each other, the second in a situation where anger would be understandable. Impose a condition that this anger is *not* to be conveyed through shouting. An example might be:

1. An athlete asks a shoe shop assistant for advice on a new pair of trainers.
2. The athlete returns to the shop after the trainers have fallen to pieces on their first outing.

Record the conversations, then play them back asking the children to note the differences in vocabulary, sentence types (relative numbers of questions, statements and imperatives, for example), interruptions, repetitions, silences and conversation markers.

The different ways in which the children represent angry language can lead to a discussion of the different ways in which it is expressed in real life, ranging from silence, through monosyllabic and over-emphatically polite speech, to incoherent raving. Each of these varieties uses words and sentence patterns in ways that the children can be encouraged to specify. A comparision of the various language styles used to express anger by the characters in a series like *Fawlty Towers* would make an interesting follow-up study.

7. Words about talk

Age range
Five to eight.

Group size
The whole class.

What you need
Shared writing materials, display board.

Curriculum context
A discussion activity that could form part of your preparations for a topic about talking.

What to do.
Ask the children for all the words, phrases and sayings that they can think of related to speech. Write the words down as the children say them, and contribute items yourself. When the children begin to dry up, suggest ways in which the words might be sorted. For example:
- Types of speech noise
whisper, shout, croak, mutter, mumble, whinge...
- Things people do with speech
discuss, announce, converse, gossip, tell news, lie...
- Sayings about speech
talk rubbish, spit it out, own up, speak up, speak out...

This can be displayed on an illustrated poster and added to as the children remember or encounter fresh examples. It will act as a reminder to the children of the great diversity of speech that surrounds them.

Oral discourse

8. Speech in writing

Age range
Six to eleven.

Group size
Small groups, then pairs.

What you need
Writing materials; tape recorders; extracts from comic strips, play scripts and dialogues from published stories.

Curriculum context
Media education, story-telling and drama.

What to do
Give each group an example of a comic strip, a play script and a story dialogue. Talk to the children about the different conventions used for representing speech in each of these media. You might raise the following points:
• Speech marks in story dialogue serve much the same function as the balloon in comic strips.
• Comic strips are usually much more flexible in their use of typography to represent the tone of an utterance.
• The tone of story dialogue can be represented by italics, exclamation marks, the choice of verb outside the speech marks (*murmured, howled, sobbed*) and by adverbs (*hurriedly, shyly, quietly*).
• Play scripts usually lack these devices (to give the actors more scope?) although they sometimes include adverbs as stage directions before the words to be spoken.

When the children are familiar with these conventions, ask them to work in pairs to compose a dialogue on some topic of current interest. When a final version has been agreed, this can be tape-recorded and transcribed into the three different media. If the earlier drafts of the conversation are also tape-recorded, this will enable the children to see the big differences between the features of spontaneous conversation and the 'unnatural' tidiness of the published conversations that they have been working with.

Further activity
You could try asking older children to make up their own conventions for transcribing speech with all of its untidinesses. A sample of a piece of conversation transcribed with arrows to indicate intonation patterns might provide some inspiration.

9. Sports/weather commentary

Age range
Six to eleven.

Group size
A small group.

What you need
Audio or video tapes of sports and weather broadcasts from radio and television.

Curriculum context
Media education and drama.

What to do
Ask the children to listen to and/or watch the tapes, noting the following points:
- nouns, verbs, adjectives and adverbs which are typical of this type of broadcast. The words in the table may be typical of a weather report;
- longer distinctive features, such as clichés and introductory and concluding phrases – 'Cricket, and another disappointing day...'; 'Can he do it?';
- differences and similarities between the language styles of the presenters.

The children can then try improvising their own broadcasts, incorporating some of these features, but also trying to subvert or individualise them. The children might be better motivated if you suggest some improbable context for the broadcast, such as a weather forecast predicting the end of the world.

10. Soap opera dialogue

Age range
Six to eleven.

Group size
A small group, working in pairs.

What you need
A short video extract from any soap opera that the children are likely to be familiar with, featuring a conversation between two people.

Curriculum context
Media education.

What to do
Show the children the extract, but keep the sound turned down. Ask them to note the clues by which one can guess at what is being said; for example, facial expression, body language and gesture. Draw their attention to the turn-taking pattern in the dialogue and how this is signalled by close-ups and cuts. These clues might also indicate conversational features like questions, statements, exclamations, commands and response signals like *yes, hmm* and *I see*.

Ask the children to make up a dialogue which will fit the visual pattern you have shown them. If the children are already familiar with the specific extract that you have

Nouns	Verbs	Adjectives	Adverbs
front	edging in	miserable	gradually
	sweeping across	sunny	slowly
depression		scattered	rapidly
heatwave	pushing (its) way		
isobars	dispersing	intermittent	continuously

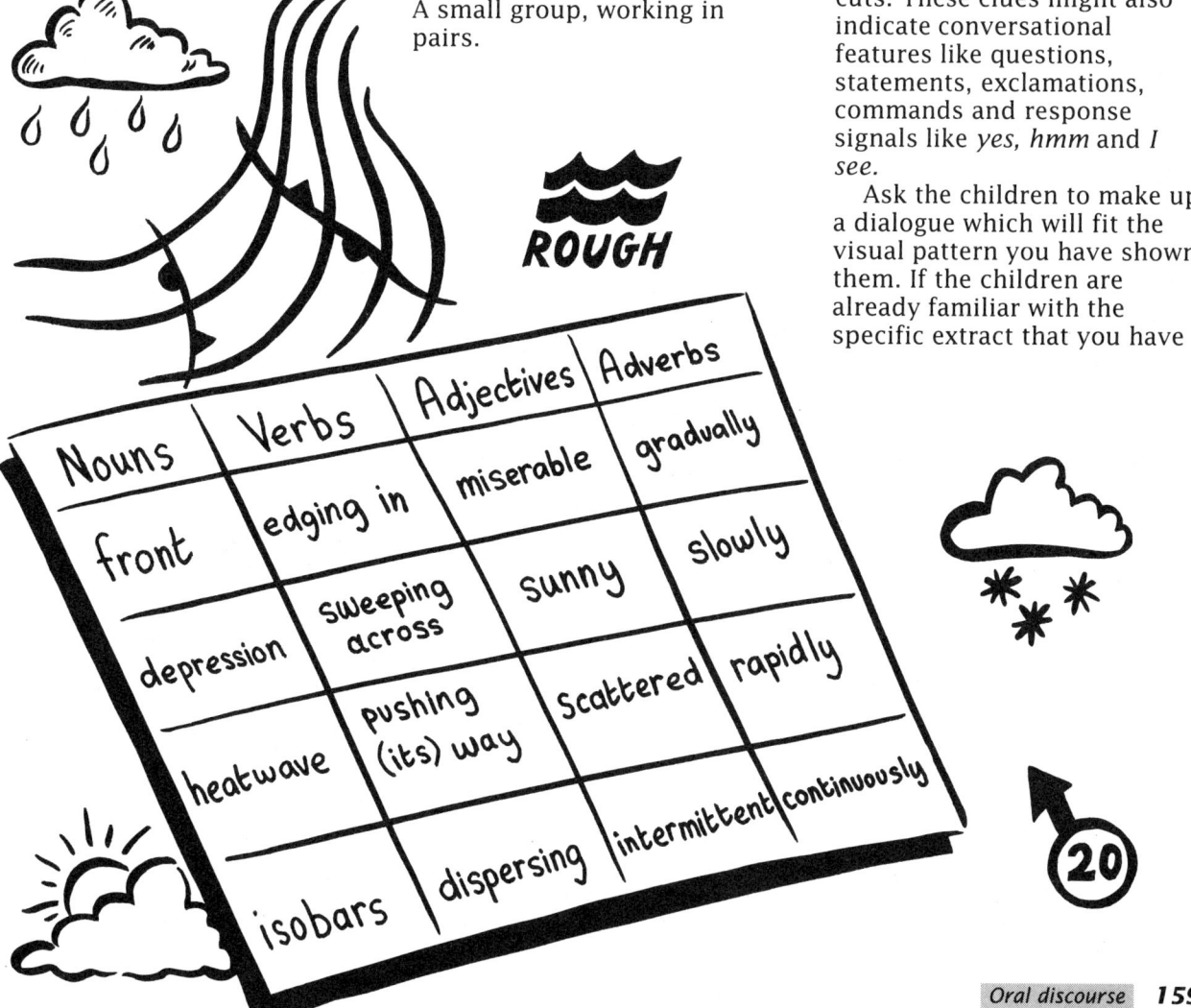

Oral discourse 159

chosen, ask them to make up an alternative that fits the same pattern. They may find it amusing to construct dialogues which are extremely untypical of the characters depicted. When the dialogues have been completed, the children can compare them with the scriptwriter's version.

11. Phone dialogue

Age range
Seven to eleven.

Group size
Pairs.

What you need
A tape recorder, writing materials.

Curriculum context
A topic on communication or drama.

What to do
You will need to seek the co-operation of the school secretary for this activity. If this is granted, set up the tape recorder in the office and collect a selection of telephone conversations (you will, of course, only be recording the secretary's half of the conversations). Choose two or three short extracts and transcribe them, bearing in mind that one minute of speech will take at least ten minutes of writing. Give the children the edited tape and transcriptions and, after they have examined them, discuss such features as:
- the use of business-like formulae (*Good morning, Plato Primary. Who's speaking please?*);
- the use of conversational 'helpers' like *yes, I see, really?*
- the use of pronouns and other referring words (collectively known as pro-forms) representing items in the other person's side of the conversation (*Is it? I can't help you with that; You'll have to choose one or the other*).

Ask the children to compose and record the missing halves of the conversations, paying careful attention to these features. Identifying workable referents for the pro-forms is likely to pose the most interesting problem; clues may be found in the emotional tone of the secretary's responses (concerned, perplexed, annoyed, amused). The dialogues that result from this activity can be used in Activity 8, Speech in writing.

12. Subvert an advert

Age range
Seven to eleven.

Group size
A small group.

What you need
A video tape of a television advertisement for any product.

Curriculum context
Media education.

What to do
Play the tape to the children and ask them to think about how the advertiser uses language. The following questions might be useful:

- What are the intended effects of the nouns, verbs, adjectives and adverbs that the advertiser uses?
- How are these words reinforced by images?
- What is the balance between information and persuasion in the advert?
- Are devices like questions and imperatives used to elicit a response from the viewer?
- Are particular accents or dialects used in order to create an effect?

When the children have discussed these points, help them to write their own script to accompany the same set of images, but this time alter the intention of the advert. For example, an advertisement for chocolate can be re-scripted into an appeal for a healthier diet; an advertisement for a powerful car turned into a road safety broadcast; an advertisement for a new type of toy might become a warning against wasting pocket money.

Consideration of how the vocabulary could be altered might provide the first step in this process. The table shows how this might be done for a chocolate advertisement.

Old advert	New advert
Nouns cocoa beans flavour energy	**Nouns** sugar additives tooth decay
Verbs enjoy enrich unwrap	**Verbs** rot avoid over-indulge
Adjectives luscious tempting creamy	**Adjectives** fattening expensive gross
Adverbs smoothly crunchily excitingly	**Adverbs** sickeningly excessively disturbingly

13. Say what you mean

Age range
Seven to eleven.

Group size
A small group working in pairs.

What you need
Cartoons illustrating situations in which politeness or professional diction conceals strong emotion.

Curriculum context
Drama.

What to do
Present the children with the cartoons and ask them to fill in the speech bubbles after acting the situation out in pairs. The situations could include:
- an air steward on his first flight confronted by a passenger with a flying phobia;
- a teacher reprimanding a year 6 child who has just knocked over an infant in the playground;
- a nervous train passenger asking a youth to turn down a personal stereo.

Discuss what they have written, then ask them to draw thought balloons alongside the speech balloons and fill in what the people are actually thinking as they speak. Compare the vocabulary and the structure of the two sets of words. They might notice that apart from obvious differences, such as the harshness of the vocabulary, or silent commands underlying spoken questions, there are interesting differences between the representation of thought and speech (see Activity 22, page 169).

The children can then be encouraged to devise, draw and script similar situations.

This activity is based on an idea from *The Languages Book* (1981, ILEA Languages Centre).

14. Conversation markers

Age range
Seven to eleven.

Group size
A small group, working in pairs.

What you need
Shared writing materials, pictures to stimulate conversation, tape recorders.

Curriculum context
Drama.

What to do
Give the children pictures showing people in conversation. Encourage them to suggest contexts for conversations by suggesting some of your own. For example:
- two old schoolfriends meet each other in the street after not seeing each other for several years;
- a stranger in a town asks a local resident about places of interest;
- a child enters the playground with some red hot gossip to share with a friend.

When a context has been decided, ask the children to improvise, rehearse and then

Openings
Hello...
Well I never!
Sorry to bother you...

Keep going words
Really?
Do you understand?
I mean to say...

Topic changers
By the way...
Speaking of that...
And another thing...

Wrapping up
Nice talking to you.
See you then.
I won't keep you.

record a conversation that fits this context. Stress that the conversation should be no more than five minutes long and must be rounded off at the end of this time.

The children can then take turns at playing back their tapes to the whole group. As they do so, put up a chart like the one shown and ask volunteers to fill in words and phrases that serve the functions mentioned. Point out that although these words and word groups do not add any information to the conversation, they serve to tie information together like function words in written sentences, and they have a vital social role to play. You can emphasise this by asking the children to improvise a conversation in which no such 'direction markers' occur.

Further activity
Children who speak languages other than English can research equivalent phrases used in these languages, and share their findings with the rest of the class.

15. Babytalk conversations

Age range
Six to eleven.

Group size
A small group.

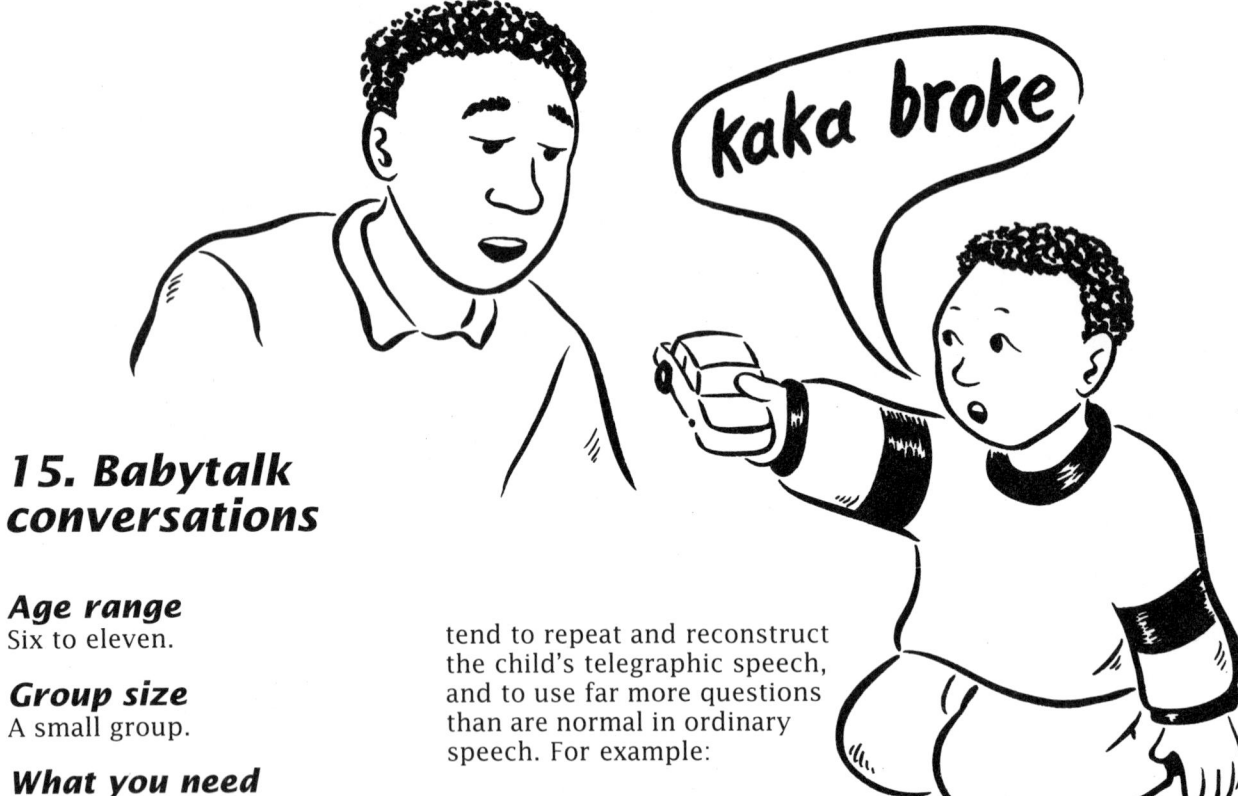

What you need
Tape-recordings and transcripts of short conversations between adults and children who are learning to talk. These can be obtained by the children themselves.

Curriculum context
A discussion activity that could be part of a topic on human development or communication.

What to do
Let the children listen to the tapes and read the transcripts, asking them to note all the ways in which these conversations differ from those between older children or adults. Draw the children's attention to the way in which adults in these conversations tend to repeat and reconstruct the child's telegraphic speech, and to use far more questions than are normal in ordinary speech. For example:

CHILD: Kaka broke.
ADULT: Your car is broken is it?
CHILD: Kaka no wheel.
ADULT: It's got no wheels? I think it still has three wheels, hasn't it?
CHILD: Make kaka better.
ADULT: Make the car better? Why don't you try to do that?

Children could discuss the purpose of this type of sentence patterning, and attempt to extend such dialogues using both young child and adult styles of sentence construction.

This activity can be related to Activity 29 in Chapter 2 (page 70) and to Activities 30 and 31 in Chapter 3 (pages 107–109).

16. One-side dialogue

Age range
Nine to eleven.

Group size
Individuals who are confident readers and writers.

What you need
Tape recorder; writing materials; tapes of comic monologues in which the comic effect relies on an implied interlocutor (for example, some of the monologues of Joyce Grenfell and Alan Bennett).

Curriculum context
A topic on communication or drama.

What to do
Play the children the tapes and ask them to try to identify what makes them funny. Point out that the speaker's words give us just enough information to reconstruct the words and behaviour of the 'absent' interlocutor. One of the most effective ways of doing this is in the use of pronouns: the listener has to guess what these words are referring to. For example:

> Put <u>that</u> down please, Adrian.
> I said put <u>it</u> down. Now, please.
> Yes, I know <u>it</u>'s an unusual specimen, but treating <u>it</u> like <u>that</u> is both dangerous and illegal.

Invite the children to compose similar monologues, reminding them that the idea is to keep the missing half of the conversation guessable, but indefinite.

17. Evasive conversation

Age range
Nine to eleven.

Group size
A small group, working in pairs.

What you need
Audio and video tapes of chat shows and political interviews; audio and, if possible, video recording equipment.

Curriculum context
Media education and drama.

What to do
Let the children watch or listen to the tapes, briefing them beforehand to pay particular attention to the ways in which the interviewee deals with unwelcome questions. They might notice the following strategies:
- ignoring the question completely;
- picking up on a word or phrase in the question and arguing about its meaning;
- rephrasing the interviewer's question and answering this self-made amendment;

Oral discourse

- asking the interviewer a counter-question;
- interrupting the interviewer part way through the question;
- answering an open-ended question with a *yes, no* or other brief response.

Invite the children to create their own interviews in which these evasions are practised. One of the pair can play the interviewer, the other can pretend to be a participant in some contemporary controversy. Record these conversations then play back the completed tapes to the rest of the class, who should try to identify the evasive strategies and to assess the effectiveness of the interviewer in dealing with them.

18. Filling the gaps

Age range
Seven to eleven.

Group size
A small group, working in pairs.

What you need
Examples of extracts from conversations in which the meaning of the words being exchanged is not immediately apparent.

Curriculum content
Drama or a topic on communication.

What to do
Drawing from your Talkhoard resource (Activity 1, page 152), give the children a conversational extract of the following type:

A: Bit breezy in here today.
B: Jane's wearing skunkjuice.
A: Sitting next to you, was she?
B: Do it yourself.

Ask the children to work out a context in which such a conversation might make sense, explaining how the situation affects the meaning to be put into the surface grammar of the utterances. For example, in the extract above, A has just entered a staffroom where B is sitting by an open window. *'Bit breezy in here'* looks like a statement but is really a request for B to close the window. B ignores the request but explains the open window: a colleague who has left the room was wearing a powerful perfume. *'Sitting next to you, was she?'* appears to be a question, but is really a repetition of the request, reminding B that he or she is nearest to the window. B again refuses the request.

The idea is not for the children to guess the actual context for such exchanges, unless they are fairly obvious, but to use their knowledge about language to construct such contexts. This activity can be presented more invitingly if the dialogue is put into disembodied speech balloons around which the children can draw the setting and participants when a context has been identified.

Children should be encouraged to spot such cryptic exchanges in the conversations that they hear around them, and to contribute them to the Talkhoard.

19. Talk for learning

Age range
Nine to eleven.

Group size
The whole class, working in groups of three or four.

What you need
A tape recorder.

Curriculum context
A communications activity that can be related to any area of the curriculum.

What to do
Tape-record the groups while they are engaged in any learning activity that involves talking; for example, exploring a new computer programme together, conducting a maths investigation or co-operating on a joint art and craft activity. At a later date, play the tapes back to the children in their groups and ask them to make notes on the following points:

• The way in which the talk is shared out between members of the group: is anyone dominant? disruptive? silent? Is there somebody providing summaries or thoughtful comments or a 'shepherd' who keeps the group on the task?
• What kinds of questions are asked? Who asks them? Who responds?
• How long are the 'turns' taken by different members of the group?
• Which parts of the talk are aimed at other members of the group and which are examples of speakers talking to themselves.
• The amount of interruption, uninterrupted speech and overlapping that occurs.

Oral discourse

When these points have been discussed, the class can reconvene and different groups can compare notes. It may be interesting to compare the characteristics of talk in single and mixed gender groups.

It is important to note that the purpose of this activity is to give children time to reflect on the complicated nature of group talk, rather than to point out their faults or to recommend a 'polite' model of discussion. Interruption, overlapping, soliloquy and meandering are natural features of group interaction, and to attempt to eradicate them would be pointless.

Further activity
Children can compare their findings from this lesson-based talk with a tape recording of children sitting at a dinner table or in the playground (you will need good equipment to obtain reasonable quality sound in these situations).

20. Parse the Lord

Age range
Nine to eleven.

Group size
A small group.

What you need
Prayers.

Curriculum context
A discussion activity that can be linked to religious education.

What to do
Take a well-known prayer like the traditional setting of The Lord's Prayer and write it, phrase by phrase, on the board. Point out that the prayer, like the conversations that they may have explored in other activities, has formulae for opening and closing the communication. Help the children to try to paraphrase what the words mean. Focus their attention on the archaic words in the text and, if necessary, supply their modern equivalents. The sentence pattens of the prayer are also interesting. What sounds like a command (*Give us this day our daily bread,* for example) is really a plea. After discussing these features, help the children to work out a translation into everyday speech. Discuss why such a translation doesn't 'sound right' as a prayer.

Further activity
The concept that certain types of language have a deliberately mysterious texture to them can be used to lead older children into a discussion of the distinctive features of certain types of professional language or jargon. Samples from legal documents, and from medical and scientific literature will help to demonstrate the 'secret code' aspect of such languages within a language.

The issues involved in exploring religious language in this way are rather sensitive, so this activity needs to be approached very carefully.

21. Inner speech

Age range
Nine to eleven.

Group size
A small group.

What you need
Pictures of people being thoughtful, writing materials.

Curriculum context
A language awareness activity that can be linked to drama.

What to do
Show the children pictures of a person in a thoughtful mood and ask them to suggest contexts. These might include:
• waiting for an important letter to arrive;
• waiting to be interviewed for a job;
• wondering how to spend a limited amount of money;
• wondering how to spend a fortune.

Ask the children to imagine themselves in one of these situations. Allow a few minutes for silent thought, then ask the children to draw speech balloons and to write inside them the exact thoughts that went through their heads during the silent period. Do the same yourself.

Oral discourse 169

Let the children compare their writing and discuss any distinctive features that they find. They might notice that representations of thought as inner speech tend to be 'telegraphic', omitting some sentence subjects and function words. For example:

Wish he'd hurry up. He's not usually this late. Must have a full sack. Or else it's a different one. Not as fast. What if it doesn't come again? Another whole day to wait. Couldn't stand that.

There is no guarantee of course that your children will choose to represent their thoughts like this. The point to make is that the degree of explicitness that a person uses is related to how much information they need to share, and how much they already share, with the person that they are talking to. If you are talking to yourself, a large amount of what you have to put into social speech can be left out.

22. One incident, many conversations

Age range
Nine to eleven.

Group size
The whole class, working in pairs.

What you need
Stimulus pictures, tape recorders, shared writing materials, sentences giving contexts for various conversations.

Curriculum context
Drama.

What to do
Present the group with the following outline, accompanied by appropriate pictures. (Photographs of people from the school community, specially posed for the occasion, would give the activity some immediacy.)

1. Two children argue in the playground at dinner time.
2. Child 1 retreats when a lunchtime supervisor intervenes but child 2 is rude.
3. A teacher arrives and tries to sort out the matter.
4. The teacher takes child 2 to the head.
5. The head tells off child 2.
6. Child 2 goes home and tells a parent about it.
7. The parent comes to see the head the next day.

Tell the children to work in pairs and to act out, rehearse and record one of the following conversations:
• child 1 and child 2;
• child 2 and the lunch-time supervisor;
• child 2 and the teacher;
• the lunch-time supervisor and the teacher;
• the teacher and the head;
• child 2 and the head;
• child 2 and the parent;
• the parent and the head.

You should ensure that the children are aware of all the different areas in which they will have to make careful language choices. The following list is not exhaustive:
• the vocabulary used by the different participants, and how this will alter depending on whom they are talking to – '*Want a scrap over it?*'/'*He challenged me to fight*';
• standard or non-standard English – '*Ain't saying sorry*'/'*I'm not sure who started it*';
• conversational markers – '*Now then, what's going on?*'/'*Have I made myself clear?*';
• the length of the sentences used, and the timing of interruptions and overlaps – '*Clearly, there has been one of those unfortunate misunderstandings that occur from time to time in any school...*'/'*I just want to know what happened*';
• the use of different name forms and of personal pronouns – '*So I told him over there to watch it!*'/'*When we've cooled down, I think we should go and see Mrs Howard, Tom*';
• the use of tenses in reporting incidents – '*There appears to have been a loss of temper*'/'*He walks up to me and thumps me*'.

The children can then share their tapes with the whole class, discussing their choices.

Further activity
This activity might provide opportunities to discuss how popular conceptions of speech styles often lead to the unfair stereotyping of characters. In subsequent activities the children can be encouraged to devise their own problem situations and to make conscious efforts to break free from such stereotyping.

Oral discourse 171

23. Speech acts

Age range
Ten to eleven.

Group size
A small group.

What you need
No special requirements.

Curriculum context
A short discussion activity to raise awareness about language beliefs and conventions.

What to do
Write the following statements on the board and ask the children if they can identify what they have in common:
- We find the defendant guilty.
- I pronounce you man and wife.
- I name this child, Andrea.
- Arise, Sir Alfred.
- You're sacked.

The interesting thing about these words is that the speaker *performs an action* merely by saying them. Ask the children to identify what each of the utterances actually does, perhaps comparing each one with a similar utterance that does not possess this power (*'I think he's guilty'*, *'Let's call her Andrea'* and so on). Talk to the children about who has the right to make such utterances and how such rights arose. Ask them to collect other examples of such speech acts and to try and find out about their history.

24. Question types

Age range
Ten to eleven.

Group size
The whole class.

What you need
Writing materials.

Curriculum context
A survey activity that could be linked to a topic on communication.

What to do
Talk to the children about the role of questions in school. Ask them to suggest different kinds of questions, what these questions are meant to do and who typically asks them. One way of doing this is to ask them to repeat as many questions as they can remember asking, being asked or overhearing in the last few days. As they do this, write the questions on the board, then help the children to sort them into categories such as the following:
- finding out who remembers what they have been told;
- finding out who knows something that they have not been told;
- getting children to think;
- questions that are really commands;
- questions that are really statements;
- questions about the running of the class.

Clearly these categories are very fuzzy, and you can expect some questions to fall into more than one category. When a format for categorising questions has been agreed, tell the children that they should attempt to find out how many of each type of question is

Oral discourse 173

actually used on a typical day in the classroom. Devise a rota system whereby the children each take a half-hour period during the day to do nothing except listen to the talk going on in the classroom, and make a tally chart of the types of questions that are asked, and who does the asking.

Naturally, in a busy classroom where the children work in groups, it would be impossible for one person to eavesdrop on all the conversations. In these circumstances, it would be better for four children to concentrate on a quarter of the classroom each. The results of such a survey could be used to discuss the variety of types of talk that go on in the classroom, who controls the talk and how this might be improved.

CHAPTER 6

Language diversity and standard English

Standard English acquired its current status through the occurrence of a combination of social and technological factors at a particular stage in the history of the language. It originated as a dialect of the East Midlands, an area that encompassed London, Oxford and Cambridge. The location of political power at London, and of prestigious seats of learning at Oxford and Cambridge, afforded this local dialect a high status, as did the relative prosperity of the inhabitants of the area enclosed by these three points.

When William Caxton set up the first English printing press at Westminster in 1476, it was inevitable that he should choose the conventions of this already prestigious dialect as the basis for his publications. Since then the vast majority of all publications in English have been in standard English. All official documents use this dialect, as well as all academic literature, national newspapers, information texts and most fiction.

With the establishment of the first American settlements in the seventeenth century, English began its phenomenal growth as a world language, a process which accelerated throughout the eighteenth and nineteenth centuries. Many countries now use English as an official language, either exclusively or in tandem with one or more other languages. These include such populous countries as the USA, India, Nigeria and the Phillippines. Most countries in which English has been adopted as a special status language have developed their own standard forms of English, differing in slight but distinctive ways from British English, although in the written mode the differences are a lot less marked.

BACKGROUND

The differences between international varieties of English is a reminder that standard English is not monolithic and immutable. The vocabulary and grammatical patterns of this dialect continue to undergo change, as does the phonology of Received Pronunciation, the accent with which it is most closely associated (see Introduction, page 12). A comparison between the news broadcasts and children's programmes of the 1950s and those of the 1990s will demonstrate this fact very effectively. The social and technological factors which caused a medieval variety of East Midlands dialect to evolve into standard English are still at work.

The status of standard English as a literary, academic and international language, coupled with its role as the language of power in this country, has implications which teachers cannot avoid. The acquisition of standard English extends the linguistic choices available to the learner: in writing, the ability to use standard English structures is essential for the production of a range of conventionally-valued texts; in speech, proficiency in this dialect (spoken in any accent) enables the speaker to adapt his or her language to the formality of the situation.

The National Curriculum demands an awareness of standard English in speaking and listening from level three, and that children should be 'usually fluent' in spoken standard English from level six. Teachers are encouraged to work from children's 'existing linguistic knowledge, drawn from oral language and their experience of reading' in order to develop competence in standard English.

Perhaps the most important role for the teacher in this process is to ensure that the child's reading provides enjoyable access to a wide range of language structures. One way of doing this is to continue to read aloud to older children from a range of texts, including good quality non-fiction which models more impersonal registers of language. The learner's encounters with standard English in reading, and practice of its structures in writing, will provide a foundation for later work in examining the role of this dialect in speech.

The National Curriculum explicitly states that 'The richness of dialects and other languages can make an important contribution to pupils' knowledge and understanding of standard English'. The idea that children should abandon the language or dialect of their home and culture in order to acquire the prestigious standard is given no support. Over a century of compulsory education, in which the received wisdom has been the superiority of standard English, has failed to establish linguistic uniformity in Britain. Broadcasting and the print media have saturated the learning environment with the patterns of standard English, but the affinities that learners have with the language of their own peer groups have proven stronger than any prescriptive attempts to impose standard English.

This is not to deny the importance of standard English or the necessity of helping children to add it to their spoken and written repertoires. However, if this is to be done successfully, we must start by respecting the child's current linguistic repertoire and cultivating curiosity about the diversity of language in general. We can do this by encouraging children to reflect on the varieties of language that they already use, demonstrating through our explorations that regional and social dialects have all the internal consistency and expressive flexibility of standard English. For many children, the repertoire might include languages other than English. It might also include language varieties like Jamaican or other Caribbean Creoles, which are historically related to English, but contain features so distinctive that they are more properly regarded as languages in their own right. Some children will have a firm command of standard English as well as any of the varieties mentioned above. All children will have repertoires of vocabulary and phraseology to be used according to the context in which they are trying to communicate.

By celebrating rather than attempting to supress such variety, we can give children confidence in their own linguistic abilities while trying to extend these abilities. We can encourage children to look beyond the language varieties they use themselves to the ways in which language, including standard English, is used by other people. As in earlier chapters, the basis of the activities which follow is the use of language in everyday life.

Issues of language use are inseparable from issues of power and authority. It is important that as well as exploring the ways in which language adapts itself to its environment, children are made aware of the strong feelings that are aroused by variation and change. We can look at the anatomical details of language variation and language contexts in the same appreciative, non-judgemental way that we can compare the structures of insect species found in different habitats. We must not forget, however, that the difference between, for example, 'we was' and 'we were' is associated with powerful belief systems about correctness in both language use and general behaviour. Accordingly, as well as encouraging children to identify instances of language variation, the activities in this chapter are aimed at getting children to explore attitudes towards these rich and fascinating phenomena.

Language diversity and standard English

ACTIVITIES

1. Many voices

Age range
Five to seven.

What you need
A tape recorder.

Group size
The whole class.

Curriculum context
A topic on language diversity, or a simple one-off game to raise children's awareness of language diversity.

What to do
Select a short, simple text such as a proverb or short poem, and ask all the children in the class, one by one, to recite it on to a tape. Children who are bilingual can be asked to record it in all the languages that they know. Play the tape back to the children and ask them to identify the speakers. Discuss the ways in which voices differ from each other.

2. Retelling

Age range
Five to seven.

Group size
Individuals or a small group retelling to the whole class.

What you need
Tape recorder, a collection of traditional tales or very short stories (*The Puffin Book of Fabulous Fables*, edited by Mark Cohen, 1989, Puffin, is a good source).

Curriculum context
An activity that can be used to draw children into your daily story-time.

What to do
After reading the class an appropriate story, invite two or three children on each occasion to retell the story to the class, using their own words. Some children will enjoy doing this, some will refuse point blank and others might be happier to do it with a small group. Tape-record the retellings, and on a later occasion, with the speakers' permission, play the different versions back to the class or to a group. The listeners can discuss points like differences in voice, vocabulary and whether or not the reteller made use of the language presented by the teacher or the original story.

3. Multilingual dictionaries

Age range
Five to seven.

Group size
The whole class.

What you need
Home-made blank 'big books', pictures of everyday objects and actions or those related to a current topic, blank labels.

Curriculum context
An open-ended, routine activity that can be used to develop vocabulary in any topic area, or used to develop awareness of language diversity and basic dictionary skills.

What to do
With younger children, you could start by asking them to name the objects on the pictures. You can then write these out on labels for the children and help them to arrange the pictures and labels in alphabetical order in the big book. You can then invite children who speak languages other than English, or whose families do, to find out what the equivalent words would be in these languages. These can then be written out by the child or teacher and the new labels added to the dictionary.

Older children could be shown how to use dictionaries of modern and ancient languages in order to research how the vocabulary of a particular area of interest (for example, food, sport or medicine) is represented in different languages. Thematic word books such as Usborne's *First 1000 Words* series are a useful source, and will show children how English words are often related to those from other languages.

4. Creole sources

Age range
Five to eleven.

Group size
The whole class.

What you need
Published material which uses Creole. Particularly appropriate for younger readers is the nursery rhyme collection *No Hickory, No Dickory, No Dock* by Grace Nicholls and John Agard (1991, Soma Books); *Caribbean Writing: A Checklist* edited by Roger Hughes (1986, Commonwealth Institute) is a useful guide to the many available titles for older readers.

Curriculum context
Reading development.

What to do
Through your selections for book display, draw the children's attention to the increasing number of books using Creole which are becoming available. Readings from this literature by Creole speakers will help to show children the characteristics of the language. Older children might be interested in the social issues surrounding the use of Creole and in its use in the work of musicians such as Bob Marley.

Language diversity and standard English

5. Dialect words

Age range
Seven to eleven.

Group size
A small group or the whole class.

What you need
Questionnaire, tape recorder, writing materials, examples of dialect words, dialect dictionary appropriate for your geographical area.

Curriculum context
A survey related to the local environment or to a topic on language diversity.

What to do
Children who speak a dialect different from standard English (in some cases this might comprise the entire class) can be asked to compile a taped or written inventory of words and expressions that do not occur (or do not occur with the same meaning) in standard English. Parents and grandparents who may use or be familiar with a local dialect can be asked to complete a questionnaire on this dialect, or they can be interviewed.

From these findings, a dictionary and grammar of the dialect or dialects can be built up. This can form the basis for discussion of the following points:
- how users of the dialects feel about the status of their dialect in comparison with standard English;
- opinions on whether any of the dialect words express ideas more or less vividly than their standard English equivalents;
- possible origins of the dialect words: many local libraries have books on local dialects that might help you to provide the children with accessible information;
- whether the dialect words are used more by one age group than another and what factors might be causing this.

6. Slang

Age range
Seven to eleven.

Group size
The whole class.

What you need
Writing materials, questionnaires.

Curriculum context
An investigation into language change and diversity.

What to do
Discuss the meaning of the term 'slang', asking the children why they think people use it. The main points to bring out are that:
- slang is a marker of identity, used to show that the speaker wants to claim membership of a particular social group;

- slang is used by all social groups;
- it is a deliberate departure from standard usage;
- professions and pastimes often have their own slang terms, which overlap with the more formal jargon, or specialised vocabulary, of that particular field;
- slang has been called 'the plain man's poetry', often expressing ideas more vividly than standard language;
- slang changes over time like any other aspect of language: some words that would have been regarded as a slang a couple of generations ago (*bus*, *zoo*, *pram* and *piano*, for example), are now accepted as standard usage.

The children can then design their own questionnaires and conduct a survey of the slang and jargon used by their families, neighbours and others. Separate questionnaires can be given to parents and grandparents to gain an impression of change over time. Some suggested starting points for a slang survey are:
- finding out all the words that people know for basic terms like *food, money, to die, to eat, good* and *bad*;
- compiling an inventory of greetings, goodbyes, insults and compliments;
- listing all the specialised words and phrases used by people when they are at work. Children can exchange such lists and try to guess what the job is;
- using dialect maps or corresponding with other schools to find out words used for basic terms in different parts of the country;
- asking bilingual children to research the slang of other languages they know.

7. Wordplay slangs

Age range
Six to eleven.

Group size
The whole class.

What you need
Tape recorders.

Curriculum context
A topic on language diversity.

What to do
Show the children examples of slang based on wordplay, such as rhyming slang and backslang.

In rhyming slang items are named by phrases that rhyme with the conventional word.

Language diversity and standard English

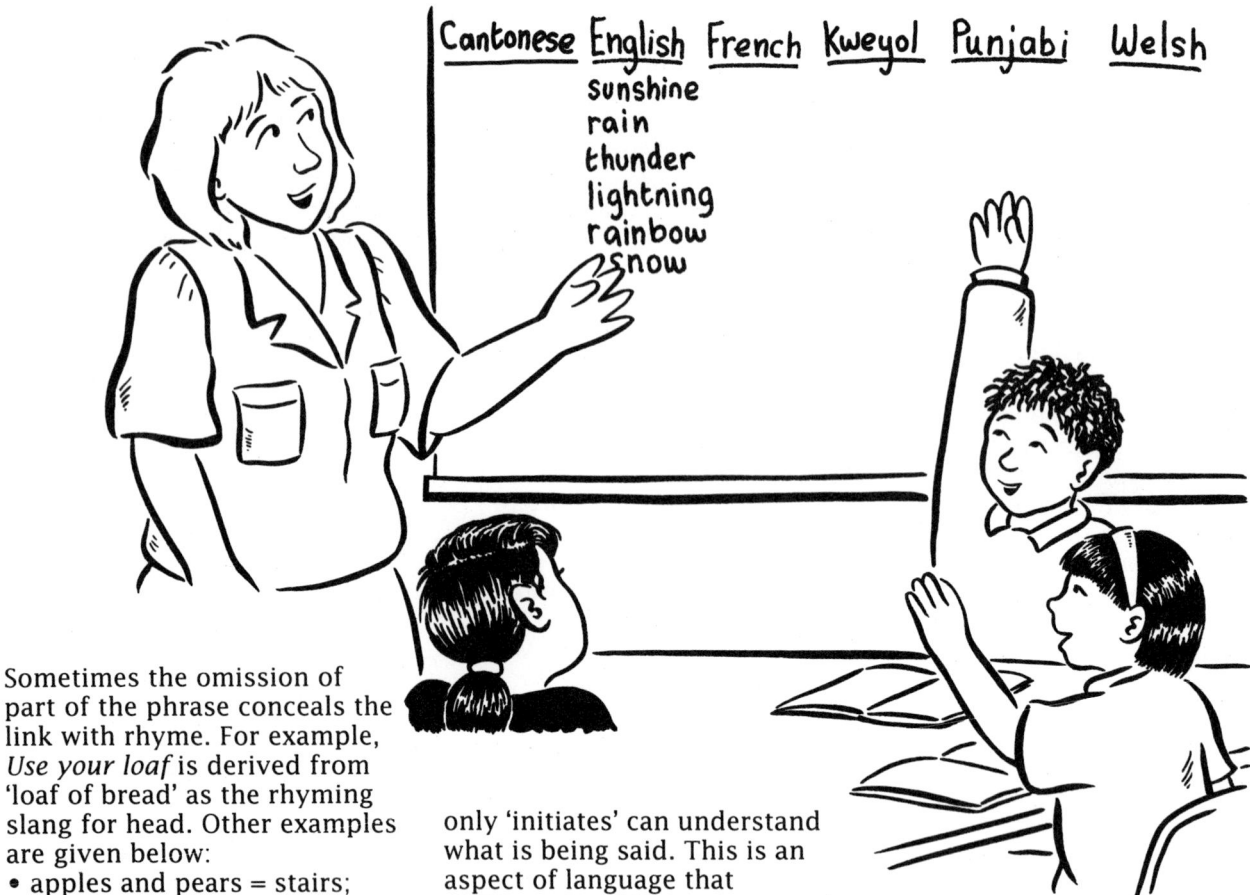

Sometimes the omission of part of the phrase conceals the link with rhyme. For example, *Use your loaf* is derived from 'loaf of bread' as the rhyming slang for head. Other examples are given below:
- apples and pears = stairs;
- Cain and Abel = table;
- God forbids = kids;
- Hampstead Heath = teeth;
- north and south = mouth;
- tea leaf = thief.

Children could use this system to invent their own terms.

In backslang, words are spelled and pronounced backwards. Some variants of this system shuffle the spellings of words and attach nonsense syllables like *ay* to the end of each word. For example, *Histay sihay nahay zamplehay fohay igpay atinlay*.

Again, children might enjoy working out the rules of such codes, exchanging messages and making up their own systems. Rhyming slang and backslang provide particularly vivid examples of the excluding function of slangs: only 'initiates' can understand what is being said. This is an aspect of language that children should be encouraged to discuss.

8. Cross-linguistic vocabulary survey

Age range
Five to eleven.

Group size
The whole class.

What you need
Formats of the type shown above.

Curriculum context
A simple survey of language diversity and similarity that can be related to any topic or subject area.

What to do
Give the children a list of words related to a current topic or subject area. Then ask them to find the equivalent terms in as many different languages as they can. Sources for this information can be the home languages of children who are bilingual or have bilingual people in the family, older brothers and sisters studying languages at secondary school or college, modern language dictionaries and phrase books such as Usborne's *First 1000 Words* series.

Discussion of the social and historical factors involved in the relationships between different languages might help the work in this and previous activities to go beyond the mere collecting of 'exotica'.

9. Saying and meaning

Age range
Six to eleven.

Group size
A small group.

What you need
Writing materials.

Curriculum context
An oral activity that can be extended into drama. It could form part of a topic on communication.

What to do
Write the following sentences on the board and ask the children what they have in common.
• Put the wood in the hole.
• I can feel an uncomfortable draught in here.
• Where you born in a field?

The children might be able to spot at this point that these are all different ways of saying '*Close the door*'.
Add the following to the list and ask the children if they can think of any more examples:
• Would you mind closing the door please?
• Could we have the door shut?
• Shut the door.

When all the variants have been exhausted, discuss the reasons why our language presents so many ways of communicating a simple message. Factors such as the level of familiarity between speakers, context, humour and slang should be mentioned. The children could then investigate ways of communicating other simple messages.

10. I ain't got none

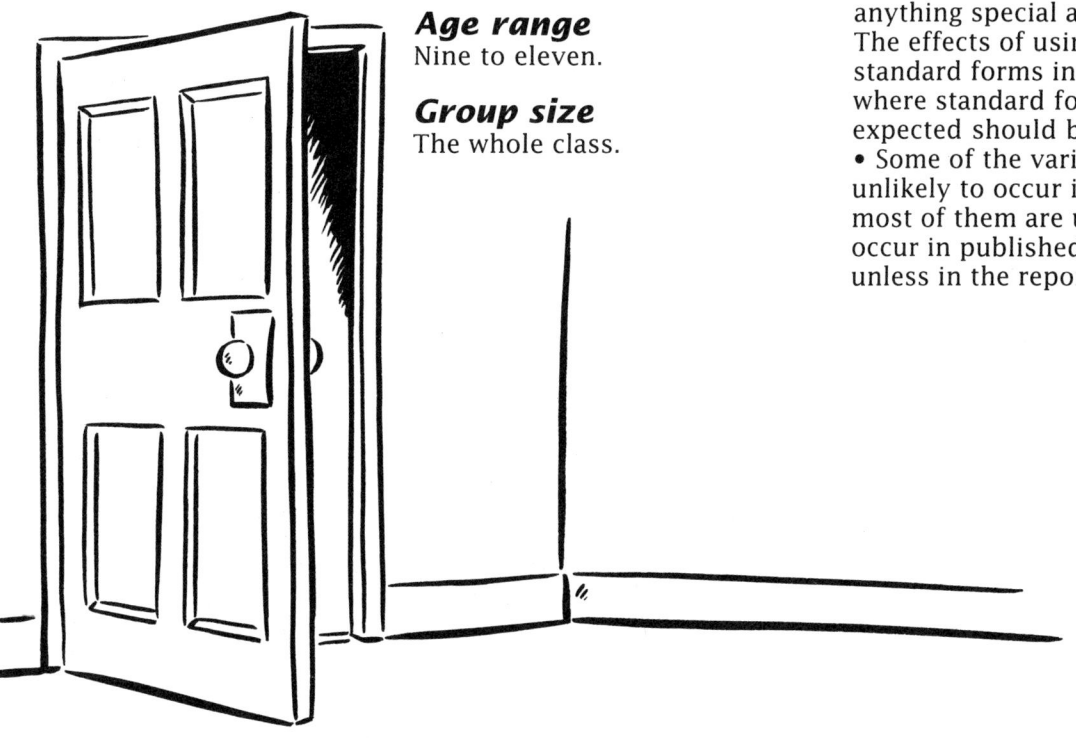

Age range
Nine to eleven.

Group size
The whole class.

What you need
Writing materials.

Curriculum context
A topic on language diversity.

What to do
Referring back to the previous activity on saying and meaning, write the following sentences on the board:
• I ain't got none.
• I ain't got any.
• I haven't got none.
• I haven't got any.
• I have not got any
• I have none.

Ask the children if they can think of any other versions of this simple message. In *Becoming Our Own Experts* (1982, Talk Workshop Group) Alex Mcleod provides a list of 18 variants. When they have all been written up, you can discuss the following points with the children.
• Of all the versions suggested, only two or three would be regarded as standard. Identify these and ask the children if they can see anything special about them. The effects of using non-standard forms in contexts where standard forms are expected should be discussed.
• Some of the variants are unlikely to occur in speech; most of them are unlikely to occur in published writing, unless in the reporting of

speech. Again, these can be identified and their distinctive features discussed.

• The children might be interested to learn that the 'rule' against double negatives is relatively recent, being another example of the work of Bishop Lowth (see Introduction, pages 7–8). Double and triple negatives occurred in Middle and Old English and can be found in other European languages. The children can compare the use of multiple negatives as intensifiers of meaning in phrases like '*no, nay, never*'. The idea that such forms are ambiguous can be tested by asking the children if anybody is likely to interpret any of the variants of '*I ain't got none*' as meaning '*I have some*'.

• The word *ain't* has a double function as a contraction of '*is not*' and '*have not*'. As a word which is commonly regarded as the epitome of 'bad English', it is sometimes used by standard English speakers to give humourous emphasis to a denial. In *Words in Time* (1989, Blackwell) Geoffrey Hughes provides an interesting history of the word that you could share with the children.

11. SV relationships

Age range
Ten to eleven.

Group size
The whole class.

What you need
Writing materials.

Curriculum context
A discussion activity that could form part of a topic on language diversity.

What to do
Remind the children of any work that they have already done on dialect variation, and tell them that the purpose of this activity is to investigate another way in which some dialects differ from standard English.

Write the following frame on the board.

I	walk	every day
You		
He		
We		
They		

Ask the children to think about how, if at all, the verb varies according to the subject when these sentences are used in their own normal speech. When is *-s* added, and when is it omitted? There is a danger, of course, that children who would normally use dialectal forms will simply give you the standard English version of the verb form on the assumption that you are asking them for 'correct' usage. A working knowledge of the local dialect on your part is essential here.

The children's answers will vary according to the area in which you teach. In many schools, different patterns will surface amongst children in the same class, as dialects vary by social background as well as by location. This fact underlines the importance of stressing that the purpose of the activity is to identify variations in language, rather than correct and incorrect forms, although the issue of prejudice against non-standard forms should be honestly addressed.

When one or more local patterns have been established, these can be set out and compared with standard English. In schools where children normally use standard English, show the children the equivalent pattern in a non-standard dialect (see table).

East Anglia	Bristol	Standard
I walk You walk He/She walk We walk They walk	I walks You walks He/She walks We walks They walks	I walk You walk He/She walks We walk They walk

You should then discuss whether standard and non-standard forms differ in meaning, consistency or intelligibility. The discussion can be extended by investigating how standard and non-standard patterns express different tenses.

Further aspects of the complexity of the so-called subject-verb agreement in standard English can be illustrated by referring to such anomalies as '*I am, aren't I?*' (compare the Scottish '*amn't I?*'), and the flexibility shown in sentences like:

Our football team *is* the best in the North.
Our football team *are* always criticising each other.

Further activity
The general strategy of identifying patterns in local dialects and comparing them with equivalent structures in standard English can be used as a regular discussion activity. A valuable resource for such work is the inventory of non-standard dialect features complied by Jenny Cheshire and Viv Edwards, which is reproduced in *Teaching Grammar* by Richard Hudson (1992, Blackwell).

Language diversity and standard English

12. Statements game

Age range
Ten to eleven.

Group size
The whole class, working in pairs.

What you need
A set of cards containing statements related to language diversity (see photocopiable page 207).

Curriculum context
A discussion activity that could introduce a topic on language diversity.

What to do
Give each pair of children a set of the cards. Ask them to read the statements and, after discussing them, to arrange them in three piles: those with which they agree, those with which they disagree and those which they are unsure of. When they have done this, each pair should compare their allocations with another pair. This should lead to further discussion and perhaps to a reallocation of some of the cards. When time has been allowed for this, each group of four can report back to the whole class.

It should be stressed that the purpose of this activity is not to come to any conclusions, but to raise various issues in the children's minds and to provide a groundwork for planning future language awareness activities. Those statements which involve questions which can be addressed through classroom and community research should be highlighted, and ways of planning such research should be discussed with the children.

This activity is based on the work of the National Oracy Project.

13. Identifying participants from speech patterns

Age range
Five to eleven.

Group size
The whole class.

What you need
Tapes and transcripts of speech that is characteristic of a particular profession; tape recorder.

Curriculum context
A topic on occupations.

What to do
Talk to the children about the jobs done by adults that they know, and ask them if they are aware of any special words or ways of talking that are related to these jobs.

Give the children the tapes and/or transcripts that you have prepared, and see if they can identify the people likely to use this language. Some examples may be:

What can you get for a pound these days? I'll tell what you can get for a pound! You can get these lovely china mugs – half a dozen and not a chip between them. Who'll give me a pound for half a dozen lovely china mugs?

Open wide. Been quite a while since we've seen you, hasn't it? Bit wider. Oh dear. We've got quite a bit to do in there, haven't we?

We'll be climbing for the next twenty minutes or so then cruising at a height of twenty eight thousand feet. You can expect a little turbulence as we go over Nova Scotia...

Ask the children to contribute their own experiences of such distinctive speech styles to a classroom talk collection.

14. Attitudes survey

Age range
Ten to eleven.

Group size
A small group.

What you need
Writing materials, a copy of *Attitudes to English Usage* by W.H. Mittins *et al.* (1979, OUP).

Curriculum context
A research activity on language awareness.

What to do
Refer back to any previous work the children have done on language diversity or attitudes towards language. Ask them to talk about any occasions on which they have had their language 'corrected' or any occasions on which they have felt like 'correcting' other people's speech.

Introduce the Mittins survey, explaining that it was an attempt made in the 1960s to assess attitudes towards non-standard language, and that many of the examples it included are now quite acceptable.

Help the children to devise a new inventory of words and phrases that they have heard people complaining about. When this has been done, they can conduct a survey on the model of the Mittins survey. The results could be published as a feature in a school magazine and would probably lead to widespread discussion.

15. Language and dialect literature survey

Age range
Nine to eleven.

Group size
Small groups.

What you need
Statistical information on the number of languages spoken by children at your school or

".... cruising at a height of twenty eight thousand feet......"

Language diversity and standard English

by their families; reading resources (mainly books but also taped books, magazines and newspapers from the school and the local library). A local children's librarian, dialect scholar or representative from a mother tongue support group would be useful here.

Curriculum context
A library survey activity that could form part of a book week.

What to do
Present the children with the information on the number of languages spoken at the school, preferably in a simple form like a pie chart or a block graph. Now help the children plan a survey of the school library to find out how well your reading resources reflect the level of diversity within the school. Small groups can take turns to scan different sections of the library, looking for books that represent different languages and dialects.

When this has been done, a report and action plan can be drawn up by the class as a whole. The local librarian and other people who know about appropriate resources could be called upon to help with this. The action plan could involve the children or members of the local community in creating resources such as taped stories and home-made books which reflect the linguistic diversity of the community (see Activity 18, page 190).

16. Reduced language

Age range
Nine to eleven.

Group size
Small groups.

What you need
Writing materials, a tape or transcript of a television weather forecast.

Curriculum context
A topic on communication.

What to do
Refer back to any activities that the children have done on telegram language or on telegraphic speech (Chapter 3, Activities 30 and 31, for example). These activities focus on situations in which language is used as *economically* as possible. Explain that a lot of features in everyday language are redundant, that is, they are not strictly necessary for the message to be understood. Write two or three sentences on the board and ask the children to identify the redundant features and remove them so that the sentence is reduced to its simplest form. For example, '*We are going to Sayers Croft on July 12th*' can be reduced to '*We go Sayers Croft July 12th*'. The same information has been conveyed in fewer words.

Ask the children to identify which parts of the original message have been declared redundant. In the example above these are:
• the auxiliary verb *are* and the verb ending *-ing*. The time framing function of these verb features is redundant, because the date is given;
• the prepositions *to* and *on*. Again, these function words are unnecessary as all the important information in the sentence can be communicated without them.

Give the children the tape or transcript and ask them to condense it into this reduced language, noting the features that they delete. (This activity provides an interesting context for the discussion of terminology like *tense, auxiliary, article* and *preposition*.) When this has been done, the intelligibility of the amended text can be tested on an audience from the rest of the class.

A language which has been stripped of complexities and reduced to the minimum number of words needed for communication is known as a *pidgin*. Children who are confident readers and writers might find it interesting to research the development of pidgin languages, which usually evolve when people who speak mutually unintelligible languages come into contact with each other. Suzanne Romaine's *Pidgin and Creole Languages* (1988, Longman) is an excellent source of information, while Loreto Todd's *Modern Englishes* (1984, Blackwell) contains some interesting examples.

It is important that the children realize that the popular conception of pidgin language as inferior is a simplistic one. Pidgins are creative, problem-solving adaptations to situations in which the use of conventional language is impossible.

Further activity

Reduced languages occur in some areas of life in which economical communication is essential. Children whose families own CB radios might be familiar with the codes of 'trucker talk'. Another source of interesting language patterns is the shipping forecasts broadcast on Radio Four. Ask the children to take the information given in the transcript on photocopiable page 208 and to rewrite it in conventional language. They could also compare the language patterns of the transcript with those of the television weather forecast. What are the differences and why do they exist?

Language diversity and standard English

17. Dialects in the media

Age range
Eight to eleven.

Group size
The whole class.

What you need
A home-made video compilation of extracts from news and weather reports, films, soap operas, commercials and so on; writing materials.

Curriculum context
Media education.

What to do
Tell the children they are going to study the different types of language used on television. Show them the video and then help them make notes on the different accents and dialects used.

Among the issues that could be raised as a result of this work are the following:
- the range of dialects that are represented in prestigious roles such as news-reading, voice-overs and investigative reporting;
- the associations that are suggested between social class dialects and personal qualities (many commercials, for example, still connect working-class dialects with stupidity or villainy);
- possible connections between the age of the presenters and the way they speak.

18. School language and dialect tape collection

Age range
Five to eleven.

Group size
The whole class.

What you need
Tape recorders.

Curriculum context
Story-telling and reading development: an ongoing project that could be initiated during a book week.

What to do
Invite parents, helpers, teachers and other members of the community who speak different languages and dialects to contribute a reading to the school's collection of story and poetry tapes. Many teachers who have initiated projects like this have been surprised at the wealth of oral literature, such as memorised stories, songs and poems, possessed by the people in the school community.

19. Fictional dialogues

Age range
Seven to eleven.

Group size
A small group.

What you need
Copies of children's stories that feature dialogue; writing materials.

Curriculum context
A shared reading project.

What to do
Ask the children to read two different books in which there are clear differences between the language varieties represented in the dialogues. A useful example would be a comparison between the speech of the schoolchildren in the Jennings stories and that of the schoolchildren in Bernard Ashley's stories (for example, *Dockside School Stories*, 1992, Walker). Ask the children to note the main differences between these styles and the ways the authors have represented speech. Subsequent discussion could focus on why the speech styles differ, which is the more representative of the speech used by the children doing the activity and how they themselves would represent their own conversations.

Language diversity and standard English **191**

20. Variation over time

Age range
Seven to eleven.

Group size
A small group or the whole class.

What you need
Videos of news broadcasts and children's programmes from the 1950s; videos of similar broadcasts from the present day. (Both *Pathe News* and *Watch with Mother* programmes are now widely available on video.)

Curriculum context
A topic in media education or language diversity.

What to do
Show the children one contemporary and one 'archival' video, matching them as closely as possible for content. Help the children to list all the similarities and differences that they notice between them. At first, the discussion will probably focus on changes in technology and fashion rather than on language. When the children do start to reflect on the language used by the presenters, allow them to list their first impressions before replaying the tape, pausing it at appropriate moments in order to discuss specific points such as accent, dialect and vocabulary.

This activity provides an interesting context for discussing the process of language change and attitudes towards it, as well as an opportunity to introduce appropriate terminology.

CHAPTER 7

Assessment and record keeping

The preceding chapters have presented activities based on a view of grammar as a system of choices available to the speaker and writer at different levels of language, from letter patterns, through words and sentences, to longer stretches of discourse. It has been emphasised that the exercise of these choices should take place in communicative contexts, and be rooted in the creation or exploration of a variety of authentic texts.

The assessment of grammatical competence should therefore be integrated with the assessment of overall language performance in these contexts. Attempts to assess such competence through decontextualised exercises have had a long and dismal history. Indeed, the weaknesses of these approaches are so striking that they have achieved official recognition. The Lockwood report, 1964, criticised the use of decontextualised grammar questions on the grounds that they failed to give an accurate picture of children's language abilities, and led to bad effects on teaching. In 1989, the Cox report recommended that assessment procedures in English should be designed to resemble normal classroom activities and that there should be no separate testing of strands within attainment targets. In the current National Curriculum for English, language study does not form a separate attainment target and is therefore not separately assessed. However, it does underlie many of the statements of attainment in speaking and listening, reading and writing.

If assessment is to be based on the child's day-to-day language use rather than on specialised exercises, procedures need to be developed to enable the teacher to focus on the child's best work. The kind of structured observation and record-keeping required by this form of assessment is already a familiar part of classroom life for many teachers. Collecting dated and annotated samples of written work in personal portfolios and making tape recordings of interesting examples of the child's conversations, have become widespread practices, partly as a result of the demands of the National Curriculum. Predating the National Curriculum, the development of the Primary Language Record (Barrs *et al.*, 1988, CLPE) by the Inner London Education Authority has familiarised many thousands of teachers with a set of procedures for formative and summative assessment which are closely based on the individual child's day-to-day talking, listening, reading and writing. The PLR methodology is based on regular sampling of the child's language use in a variety of contexts. These samples are then used to create a profile reflecting growth of competence over time and across a variety of social and curricular contexts. It is this model of assessment which underlies the suggestions in the rest of this chapter. Some guidelines for assessment procedures are suggested below.

Sample from as wide a variety of contexts as possible.

One of the themes running through this book is that different contexts require different types of language. The vocabulary and structure suitable for a science report are not the same as those required for recounting an episode in a letter to a friend. The type of talk involved in telling a story is not the same as that required for contributing to a discussion. By taking samples of language from as wide a variety of contexts as possible, we can try to ensure that strengths which are not evident in one episode have a chance to show themselves in another. We can also help to iron out short-term inconsistencies in performance caused by shifts of mood and motivation.

Make assessment a normal, unobtrusive part of the school day.

Distortions in children's behaviour can occur if they feel they are being tested or eavesdropped on. They tend to use what the sociolinguist Labov has referred to as 'careful' rather than 'spontaneous' language. If tape-recording and the creation of portfolios of written work become routine activities in the classroom, the children are less likely to respond to these procedures with anxiety or a counter-productive desire to put on their best linguistic table manners.

Involve children in assessment procedures.
Children should be made explicitly aware of the general principles by which the teacher judges their performance. These can be expressed as a set of questions that the children can consult occasionally in order to assess their own performance.

In order to involve children in longitudinal assessment, many teachers have introduced them to the use of journals in which they can reflect on their own talking and writing. (Publications from the National Writing Project and the National Oracy Project provide many valuable suggestions along these lines.) Children can also be involved in selecting and annotating pieces of written work to be added to a personal portfolio which is compiled and edited throughout their years at primary school. Some teachers of younger children have found it helpful to append to such collections a set of statements, written with the child, setting out what the writing demonstrates about that child's abilities. As the number of statements increases, the child gets a clear impression of his or her own growing competence.

Focus on process as well as product.
The processes that the learner goes through in shaping a piece of work are often more informative than the work itself. The linguistic strategies involved in the shaping of writing may include note-making, the tentative use of speech in adopting and adapting a partner's suggested amendments, and the refinement of vocabulary and sentence structure during redrafting. To get a fuller picture of a learner's abilities, observations of children's discussions and of their struggles with the developing text are essential. What the child leaves out is as informative as what is presented. The ability to distil a few telling notes from a complex text or to delete adjectives from a first draft are important ones, but not immediately obvious in the finished products.

Focus on overall communicative effect rather than on subskills.
The main question to ask when assessing samples of speech or writing is 'Does this piece of language do the job that it was intended to do?' Although it can be helpful to have a checklist of subskills to look for in the sample, the main concern is the way such subskills are orchestrated in order to produce an effect appropriate for audience and purpose. A story consisting of a series of well-constructed and immaculately punctuated sentences in optimum order might earn a whole column of ticks on a checklist, yet still bore its intended readers rigid.

Be wary of equating the use of grammatical complexity with linguistic ability.
This point is closely linked to the previous one. Although progress in the ability to handle increasingly complex structures is to be welcomed and encouraged, complexity is not synonymous with quality. If it were, we might rank the language of a legal document above that of a skilled story-teller. To take other examples, it is the linguistic simplicity of a proverb or of an effective one-word contribution to an argument that gives these forms of expression their power. In the classroom, a child writing notes, a set of instructions or a story for a younger audience, may use simple or abbreviated structures that are far more appropriate to the task in hand than complex sentences. Again, it all depends on what the learner is trying to do with the language.

Look beneath the surface features of language.
When we look at a piece of work, it is often the errors and flaws in presentation that strike us first. Significant linguistic achievements can be missed unless we are willing to look beyond these surface features to the deeper aspects of the language, such as the child's handling of sentence and discourse structures. The following example from Katherine Perera in *Children's Writing and Reading* (1984, Blackwell, p.267) vividly illustrates this point:

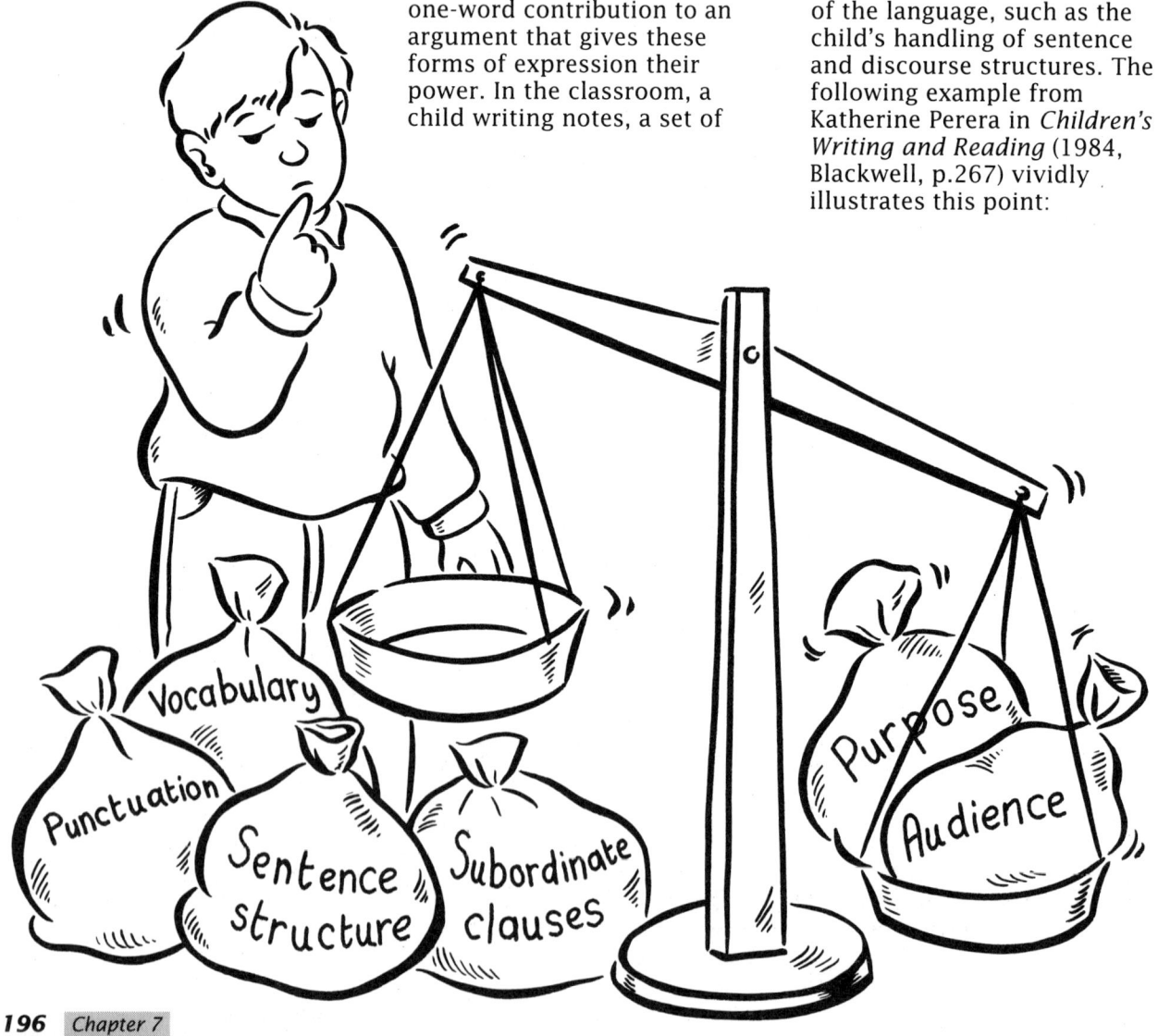

the following extract, given in its original spelling, ends a short letter asking a farmer to buy a puppy:

...he is very playful with people I just got read of five I can not keep it so I folt of you becauese I no you are got with animals
(Peter, 9 years)

Although they are not marked by punctuation, the three sentences in this extract are all well formed and there is no difficulty in deciding where the full stops should go. Then the last sentence, with its three competently managed subordinate clauses, provides a strong ending to the letter.

The tendency to focus on error rather than achievement can be particularly distorting when teachers are assessing spoken language. Many of the 'errors' that people make in spontaneous speech are natural phenomena that a listener focusing on meaning would barely notice (see Chapter 5). It is also important that teachers who do not speak the same dialect as their children should strive to become familiar with the structures of this dialect so that they are not mistaken for speech errors.

Be aware of different types of error in written work.
Try to avoid the tendency to treat all deviations from correctness in a uniform manner. Perera *(ibid)* suggests that errors might be classified in the following ways:

At sentence level
1. Errors caused by haste and inadequate proof-reading, such as omissions, repetitions and the conflation of different sentence patterns.
2. Errors caused by the pupil experimenting with unfamiliar constructions.
3. The use of dialect expressions that might not be appropriate in certain forms of writing.
4. The use of constructions which are normal in speech but less acceptable in writing.

At discourse level
5. Inconsistent use of pronouns and tense sequences.
6. Omissions of major structural components such as introductions or conclusions.
7. Muddled sentence order, particularly in non-chronological texts.
8. Inappropriate overall response, as when a child uses a narrative style in writing a science report.

Assessment and record keeping 197

These categories provide a valuable framework for differentiating our responses to children's work. Errors of types 1, 5, 6 and 7 for example, might best be addressed by giving children practice in co-operative proof-reading and editing skills, whereby writing partners check each others' first drafts for features like overall coherence, tense consistency and unambiguous pronoun usage. Children making errors of types 3, 4 and 8 might benefit from activities which explore differences between spoken and written texts, the role of standard English and the distinctive features of different genres. Errors of type 2 in a child's work should, of course, be welcomed as a sign of the risk-taking that accompanies progress in grammatical development. The child will need help to use the new construction correctly, but the teacher's first response should be congratulation.

Value what children bring to the classroom.

Traditionally, assessment has been seen as a set of procedures for measuring how effective school experience has been in stocking the child's intellect with the goods offered by the curriculum. In the case of language, these goods might consist of competence in an ever-widening variety of linguistic structures and conventions, from the correct spellings of common words to the ability to express meaning in a variety of spoken and written genres.

However, if children are to be encouraged to build confidently on their intuitive knowledge of language, it is vital that status be given to those aspects of language that are not explicitly taught by the school, and do not feature in any official curriculum. These might include oral story-telling ability, idiosyncratic repertoires of words, phrases and sayings built up from personal and family experience and, above all, the diversity of dialects and languages that the children bring to the school from their own homes and cultures.

CHAPTER 8

Bibliography

Adams, M.J., *Beginning to Read* (1990, MIT Press)

Aitchison, J., *Words in the Mind* (1987, Blackwell)

Ashton Warner, S., *Keywords* (1963, Simon & Schuster)

Barrs, M. et al., *The Primary Language Record Handbook* (1988, CLPE)

Botkin, B.A., *A Treasury of American Folklore* (1944, Crown Books)

*Brownjohn, S., *Does it have to Rhyme?* (1980, Hodder & Stoughton)

*Brownjohn, S., *What Rhymes with Secret?* (1982, Hodder & Stoughton)

Crystal, D., *Cambridge Encyclopaedia of Language* (1987, CUP)

Czerniewska, P., *Learning About Writing*, (1992, Blackwell)

DES/Welsh Office, *English in the National Curriculum* (1990, HMSO)

DES, *English 5–16* (1984, HMSO)

DES, *Report of the Committee of Inquiry into the Teaching of the English Language* (Kingman Report) (1988, HMSO)

DES/Welsh Office, *English for Ages 5–16* (Cox Report) (1989, HMSO)

Dunkling, L. and Gosling, W., *Dictionary of First Names* (1983, Dent)

Gentry, R.R., 'An Analysis of Developmental Spelling' in *GYNS AT WRK* (November 1982, The Reading Teacher)

Gentry, R.R., *SPEL is a Four Letter Word* (1982, Scholastic)

*Goddard, A., *The Language Awareness Project* (1989, Framework Press)

Gowers, E., *The Complete Plain Words* (1962, Pelican)

*Hudson, R., *Teaching Grammar* (1992, Blackwell)

Hughes, M., *Words in Time* (1988, Blackwell)

Hughes, R., *Caribbean Writing: A Checklist* (1986, Commonwealth Institute)

Manser, M.H., *Dictionary of Eponyms* (1988, Sphere Books)

Mcleod, A., 'Writing, Dialect and Linguistic Awareness' in *Becoming Our Own Experts* (1982, Talk Workshop Group)

Mittins, W.H. et al., *Attitudes to English Usage* (1979, OUP)

Opie, I. and Opie, P., *Children's Games in Street and Playground* (1984, OUP)

Oxford Dictionary of English Etymology (1966, OUP)

Oxford Dictionary of English Proverbs (1970, OUP)

Partridge, E., *Usage and Abusage* (1973, Penguin)

Perera, K., *Children's Writing and Reading* (1984, Blackwell)

Perera, K., *Understanding Language* (1987, National Association of Advisers in English)

*Peters, M. and Smith, B., *Spelling in Context, Strategies for Teachers and Learners* (1993, NFER/Nelson)

Peters, M.L., *Spelling, Caught or Taught? – A New Look* (1990, Routledge)

*Raleigh, M., *The Languages Book* (1981, The English and Media Centre)

Romaine, S., *Pidgin and Creole Languages* (1988, Longman)

*Shepherd, V., *Playing the Language Game* (1993, Open University Press)

Smith, Frank, *Writing and the Writer* (1982, Heinemann Educational)

Todd, L., *Modern Englishes* (1984, Blackwell)

WORLDAWARE, *Songs, Games and Stories from Around the World* (A cassette and booklet are available from WORLDAWARE, The Centre for World Development Education, 1 Catton Street, London WCR 4AB.)

Further reading

All titles above which are marked with an asterisk contain practical ideas for developing knowledge about language, as well as further information about the issues addressed in this book. The following titles should also be useful.

Andersson, L. and Trudgill, P., *Bad Language* (1992, Penguin)

Bain, R., Fitzgerald, B. and Taylor, M., *Looking into Language* (1992, Hodder & Stoughton)

Barber, C.L., *The Story of Language* (1982, Pan)

Carter, R. (ed), *Knowledge About Language* (the LINC Reader) (1990, Hodder & Stoughton)

Crystal, D., *Language A-Z Books 1 and 2* and *Teachers' Book* (1991, Longman)

Gregory, A. and Woolard, N. (eds), *Looking into Language Diversity in the Classroom; Support Service for Language and Intercultural Education, Reading* (1984)

Haynes, J., *A Sense of Words* (1992, Hodder & Stoughton)

Houlton, D., *All Our Languages* (1985, Edward Arnold)

Keen, J., *The Language Awareness Project* (1989, Framework Press)

LINC, *Language in the National Curriculum: Materials for Professional Development* (1992). Obtainable from the LINC Secretary, Department of English Studies, University of Nottingham.

Open University, *Every Child's Language Multilingual Matters* (1985, Open University)

Rosen, M., *Did I Hear You Write?* (1989, André Deutsch)

Information about the work and publications of the National Oracy Project are available from Gordon Badderley, Pine Trees, Skelwith Fold, Ambleside, Cumbria, LA22 OHT

Reports on the work of the National Writing Project (*Becoming a Writer, Audiences for Writing* and *Responding to and Assessing Writing*) are published by Thomas Nelson (1989).

Dr M. Sharples at the University of Sussex has recently developed an interesting computer programme aimed at helping children to explore sentence grammar. Information on the 'Boxes' programme is available from COGS, University of Sussex, Falmer, Brighton BN1 9QH.

Children's books referred to in the text

Agard, J., *The Calypso Alphabet* (1989, HarperCollins)

Ahlberg, A. and Ahlberg, J. *The Jolly Postman* (1989, Heinemann)

Ahlberg, A. *The Ha Ha Bonk Book* (1982, Penguin)

Ashley, B., *Dockside School Stories* (1992, Walker)

Bennet, J. and Sharratt, N., *Noisy Poems* (1987, OUP)

Berenstain, S. and Berenstain, J., *Bears in the Night* (1981, Collins)

Carroll, L., *Alice Through the Looking Glass* (1989, Dragon's World)

Cohen, M. (ed), *The Puffin Book of Fabulous Fables* (1989, Puffin)

Dahl, R., *The BFG* (1982, Jonathan Cape)

Hoban, R., *How Tom Beat Captain Najork and his Hired Sportsmen* (1993, Random House)

King-Smith, Dick, *The Hodgeheg* (1989, Puffin)

Look and Wonder Series (1993, Walker)

Magee, Wes, *Madtail, Miniwhale and Other Shape Poems* (1991, Penguin)

McGough, R., *The Kingfisher Book of Comic Verse* (1986, Kingfisher)

Messenger, N., *Making Faces* (1992, Dorling Kindersley)

Morgan, Edwin, *Selected Poems* (1985, Carcanet)

Nichols, G. and Agard, J., *No Hickory, No Dickory, No Dock* (1991, Soma Books)

Ridley, P., *Dakota of the White Flats* (1989, Collins)

Sendak, Maurice, *Where the Wild Things Are* (1967, Bodley Head)

Yorke, M., *A Dormal Nay* (1987, Thomas Nelson, Story Chest Level 11)

AT CHART

This chart refers to different components of the Scottish curriculum for English covered by activities in this book. Activities are identified by chapter and activity number: **2**/3 is Chapter 2, Activity 3.

Strands	Level A	Level B	Level C	Level D	Level E
Functional writing	**3**/1; **4**/1, **4**/4, **4**/6, **4**/19-20; **6**/3, **6**/5	**3**/1; **4**/1, **4**/4, **4**/6, **4**/18-20, **4**/22, **6**/3, **6**/5-6	**3**/1; **4**/1, **4**/10, **4**/12, **4**/18-19, **4**/22, **4**/28, **4**/34; **6**/6	**3**/1; **4**/12, **4**/18-20, **4**/22, **4**/28-29, **4**/33-34; **5**/5, **5**/12, **5**/20; **6**/6, **6**/14, **6**/16	**3**/1; **4**/18, **4**/20, **4**/28-29, **4**/33-34; **5**/5, **5**/12, **5**/20; **6**/14-16
Personal writing		**3**/2; **4**/23	**4**/23, **4**/34	**4**/23, **4**/34	**4**/23, **4**/34
Imaginative writing	**4**/8, **4**/11	**4**/8-18	**4**/8-18, **4**/34; **5**/9, **5**/16, **5**/18, **5**/21	**4**/9, **4**/11-18, **4**/27, **4**/34; **5**/9-11, **5**/13, **5**/16, **5**/18, **5**/21	**4**/16, **4**/18, **4**/27, **4**/34; **5**/9-11, **5**/13, **5**/16, **5**/18, **5**/21
Punctuation and structure	**3**/2, **3**/5	**3**/5-7, **3**/14, **3**/17-18; **4**/10-11, **4**/16-18, **4**/23-25	**3**/5-6, **3**/12, **3**/14-15, **3**/17-18; **4**/10-11, **4**/16-18, **4**/22-25; **5**/8, **5**/18, **5**/21	**3**/5-6, **3**/12, **3**/14, **3**/17, **3**/19-23, **3**/29, **3**/32; **4**/16-18, **4**/22-25, **4**/27; **5**/2, **5**/5, **5**/8, **5**/10-11, **5**/13, **5**/18, **5**/21	**3**/29, **3**/32; **4**/24-25, **4**/27; **5**/8, **5**/10-11, **5**/18, **5**/21
Spelling	**1**/1-12, **1**/17, **1**/22, **1**/25; **2**/8; **6**/3, **6**/5	**1**/7-12, **1**/17-19, **1**/22, **1**/25; **2**/8-9; **3**/16, **3**/18; **6**/3, **6**/5	**1**/7-20, **1**/22, **1**/25; **2**/9; **3**/16, **3**/18; **6**/5	**1**/11-27; **2**/9	**1**/11-16, **1**/19-21, **1**/23-27; **2**/9
Handwriting and presentation	**1**/2-5, **1**/17; **2**/8	**1**/2-5, **1**/17; **2**/8; **3**/18	**3**/18		
Writing: Knowledge about language	**2**/1, **2**/3-5; **6**/3	**1**/1-3, **1**/8-12; **2**/1, **2**/3-9; **2**/12-13; **3**/1-6; **3**/8-9; **3**/11-12, **3**/14; **3**/16-17; **4**/24-25; **5**/7; **6**/3, **6**/7-9	**1**/8, **1**/10-12; **2**/1, **2**/3, **2**/5-7; **2**/9-11, **2**/13, **2**/15-18, **2**/21; **3**/4, **3**/6, **3**/8-14, **3**/16-17, **3**/19-20, **3**/27, **3**/30; **4**/18, **4**/24-25, **4**/34; **5**/7, **5**/9; **6**/7-10	**1**/23; **2**/1-3, **2**/5-6, **2**/9-11, **2**/13-22, **2**/24, **2**/29; **3**/7-17, **3**/20-32; **4**/18, **4**/24-25, **4**/27, **4**/30, **4**/34; **5**/9, **5**/12, **5**/14, **5**/18, **5**/20; **6**/7-10, **6**/14, **6**/19	**2**/2, **2**/5, **2**/9, **2**/16, **2**/18-36; **3**/13, **3**/15, **3**/21-32; **4**/18, **4**/24-25, **4**/27, **4**/30, **4**/34; **5**/9, **5**/12, **5**/14, **5**/18, **5**/20; **6**/9-11, **6**/13-15, **6**/19
Reading: Awareness of genre	**4**/2, **4**/21	**4**/2-3, **4**/21	**4**/2-3, **4**/21, **4**/34	**4**/2-3, **4**/21, **4**/31-34	**4**/2-3, **4**/21, **4**/31-34
Reading: Knowledge about language	**4**/7	**4**/4, **4**/7	**4**/4, **4**/7, **4**/26	**4**/4, **4**/26	**4**/26
Listening: Awareness of genre		**5**/1-4	**5**/1-4	**5**/1-6, **5**/14-15, **5**/23	**5**/5-6, **5**/14-15, **5**/23
Listening and talking: Knowledge about language		**6**/1-2, **6**/4-5, **6**/7-9	**6**/1-2, **6**/4-5, **6**/7-10, **6**/20	**5**/5-6, **5**/9-12, **5**/14-15, **5**/17, **5**/20, **5**/22-23; **6**/2, **6**/4-5, **6**/7-10, **6**/14, **6**/17-18, **6**/20	**5**/5-6, **5**/9-12, **5**/14-15, **5**/20, **5**/22-23; **6**/9-11, **6**/13-18, **6**/20

PHOTOCOPIABLES

The pages in this section can be photocopied and adapted to suit your own needs and those of your class; they do not need to be declared in respect of any photocopying licence. Each photocopiable page relates to a specific activity in the main body of the book and the appropriate activity and page references are given above each photocopiable sheet.

Statements game, page 186

Royal family ... better English ...ost other ...ople.	People who come to live in Britain should learn the English language.	It is wrong to drop your Hs when you're saying words like *her*, *him* and *hospital*.
Australian ...an forms ...ust as ...rieties	The English language has been improved by all the changes that have occurred over the last few years.	People who can speak both French and English are more skilful than those who can speak only English.
	Teachers should never correct the speech of children.	Teachers should never use slang words in front of children.
...en forms like '...' and 'innit' ...loppy.		
...se language ...r than boys		

Playing with spelling possibilities, page 44

Hints on Pronunciation for Foreigners

I take it you already know
Of *tough* and *bough* and *cough* and *dough*?
Others may stumble but not you
On *hiccough*, *thorough*, *laugh* and *through*.
Well done! And now you wish, perhaps,
To learn of less familiar traps?

Beware of *heard*, a dreadful word
... like *beard* and sounds like *bird*,
... like *bed* not *bead* —
... call it '*deed*'!
... *threat*
... *debt*).

Cromary Forth: southerly three or four, mainly fair, good.

Tyne/Dogger: southerly three or four, occasionally five later, rain for a time, moderate or poor, becoming good.

Fisher/German Bight: south-east veering south-west four or five, decreasing three for a time, rain or drizzle, moderate or poor.

Humber Thames/Dover Wight: southerly four increasing five later, thundery rain then showers, moderate or poor, becoming good from west.

Photocopiable pages 203

Playing with spelling possibilities, page 44

Hints on Pronunciation for Foreigners

I take it you already know
Of *tough* and *bough* and *cough* and *dough*?
Others may stumble but not you
On *hiccough*, *thorough*, *laugh* and *through*.
Well done! And now you wish, perhaps,
To learn of less familiar traps?

Beware of *heard*, a dreadful word
That looks like *beard* and sounds like *bird*,
And *dead*: it's said like *bed* not *bead* –
For goodness' sake don't call it '*deed*'!
Watch out for *meat* and *great* and *threat*
(They rhyme with *suite* and *straight* and *debt*).

A *moth* is not a *moth* in *mother*
Nor *both* in *bother*, *broth* in *brother*,
And *here* is not a match for *there*
Nor *dear* and *fear* for *bear* and *pear*,
Just look them up – and *goose* and *choose*,
And *cork* and *work* and *card* and *ward*,
And *font* and *front* and *word* and *sword*,
And *do* and *go* and *thwart* and *cart* –
Come, come, I've hardly made a start!
A dreadful language? Man alive.
I'd mastered it when I was five.

T.S.W.
From a letter published in *The Sunday Times*,
3 January 1965

Dinosaur names, page 55

tyran
ruler

cera
horn

saurus
lizard

bronto
thunder

odont
tooth

dactyl
foot

rhin
nose

platy
flat

pyr
fire

ptero
wing

mega
great

cephalus
head

ichthy
fish

xanth
yellow

pod
foot

mono
one

chloro
green

phag
eating

di
two

melan
black

phil
loving

tri
three

tachy
swift

phobe
fearing

tetra
four

anthro
human

Insults, page 60

badmash

quidnunc

gaby

cacafuego

saltimbanco

gnoss

criticaster

scobberlotcher

jackeen

dandyprat

scodgy

juggins

doddypoll

sculpin

minnick

draffsack

shifter

mumpsimus

drumble

slubberdegullion

myrmidon

fizgig

soss

persifleur

fribble

wallydrag

fustilugs

zoilus

Statements game, page 186

The Royal family speak better English than most other British people.	People who come to live in Britain should learn the English language.	It is wrong to drop your Hs when you're saying words like *her*, *him* and *hospital*.
American, Australian and Caribbean forms of English are just as good as the varieties originating in the British Isles.	The English language has been improved by all the changes that have occurred over the last few years.	People who can speak both French and English are more skilful than those who can speak only English.
You should never use a long word where a short one will do.	Teachers should never correct the speech of children.	Teachers should never use slang words in front of children.
Children don't speak as well as they did when I was a child.	People should be proud of their accents and dialects.	Spoken forms like 'ain't' and 'innit' are sloppy.
It is always wrong to swear.	People who can speak both Bengali and English are more skilful than those who can speak only English.	Girls use language better than boys do.

Reduced language, page 188

Cromarty Forth: southerly three or four, mainly fair, good.

Tyne/Dogger: southerly three or four, occasionally five later, rain for a time, moderate or poor, becoming good.

Fisher/German Bight: south-east veering south-west four or five, decreasing three for a time, rain or drizzle, moderate or poor.

Humber Thames/Dover Wight: southerly four increasing five later, thundery rain then showers, moderate or poor, becoming good from west.

208   *Photocopiable pages*